The Cranberry
COOKBOOK

YEAR-ROUND DISHES FROM BOG TO TABLE

The Cranberry
COOKBOOK

SALLY PASLEY VARGAS

Globe
Pequot

GUILFORD, CONNECTICUT

For Luke, who always brings joy to the table

Globe Pequot

An imprint of Rowman & Littlefield

Distributed by NATIONAL BOOK NETWORK

Copyright © 2017 Sally Pasley Vargas

Photos by Sally Pasley Vargas
(with the exception of those on pages vi, vii, ix, 28, 44, 60, 70, 100 © istockphoto.com)

Cover and interior design by Diana Nuhn

British Library Cataloguing in Publication Information Available

Library of Congress Cataloging-in-Publication Data available

ISBN (hardback) 978-1-4930-2809-2
ISBN (e-book) 978-1-4930-2810-8

∞™ The paper used in this publication meets the minimum requirements of American National Standard for Information Sciences—Permanence of Paper for Printed Library Materials, ANSI/NISO Z39.48-1992.

Contents

Introduction

On a recent rainy Saturday, I turned off the highway from Boston to Cape Cod to observe a cranberry harvest at a small bog in Freetown, Massachusetts. I left with a bag of gorgeous, fat, red berries and the first thing I did the following day was throw a handful of those scarlet beauties into my morning oatmeal.

Fresh cranberries are wondrous fruits. Tart as can be, they often need sugar to bring out the berry flavor. Because the season coincides with the first big fall holiday, many Americans tend to relegate cranberries to the Thanksgiving table and forget about them for the rest of the year. I hope to change your mind!

A savory roasted chicken with cranberry cornbread salad makes a cozy fall supper, and squash stuffed with berries and wild rice is perfect for the vegetarian table. You could toss a handful of cranberries into roasted carrots, add them to a salad with lentils and feta cheese, mix them with quinoa, or try cauliflower biryani, an Indian dish in which dried cranberries add a piquant element. I can't start my morning without a nutty cranberry breakfast bar when I'm racing out the door, and everyone's chocolate cravings will be satisfied with chocolate gelato and bourbon-infused cranberries, or a cranberry-chocolate tart. The fresh fruits are often unexpected in confections, and the dried berries can go into any dish that calls for raisins—and maybe I'm biased, but I think cranberries are prettier.

In my experience as a pastry chef, chef, cooking teacher, and recipe developer, I've never cooked with such an adaptable berry. You'll see in these pages of recipes and in my photographs, just how easily they transform sweets with a ping of zesty brightness and how they infuse salads and savory dishes in pleasing and unexpected ways.

When the Colonists came to the New World, they recognized the tart red berries that grew in boggy parts of England and the Netherlands. Native Americans already knew how valuable the fruits were and they found they could sell their harvest for supplies such as flour and molasses, which they did beginning in the nineteenth century. Today, the Wampanoag people on Martha's Vineyard celebrate Cranberry Day on the second Tuesday in October. As Durwood Vanderhoop of the Wampanoag Tribe of Gay Head explains it, "We get up early and the cranberry agent opens the wild bog for picking. We say prayers at sunrise, and families gather to pick and share a picnic lunch." Their scoops and rakes have been handed down for generations. Vanderhoop says it's the most meaningful of all their harvest celebrations.

Massachusetts, where I live, is one of the leading states in cranberry harvest, and the fruit is the state's most important crop. Wisconsin, New Jersey, Oregon, and Washington State are also top cranberry producers. In Massachusetts, many of the growers are in the southeast corner of the state, and sell their crop to a cooperative such as Ocean Spray, established in the early twentieth century. While there have been technological advances in harvesting methods, the growing is still done by small enterprises, oftentimes families.

Surprisingly, this doesn't typically include workers wading knee-deep in water. The fresh cranberries you find in the market represent only a small percentage of the crop and are actually dry-harvested. Until the harvest, trailing cranberry vines grow in low-lying depressions that were originally formed by glaciers. Impermeable clay on the bottom; layers of sandy soil and accumulated organic matter; and proximity to wetlands, streams, and ponds provide the ideal growing conditions for America's first fruit. The berries thrive in bogs much like wild plants, requiring occasional irrigation if they are being cultivated. The guys knee-deep in cranberries on TV are standing in flooded bogs, a practice adopted in the 1950s to facilitate the harvest. Ninety percent of all cranberries are wet-harvested for juice and dried cranberries.

All fresh or frozen berries used for cooking and baking must be dry-picked, without a trace of moisture. Forty years ago, this meant hand scooping and raking the berries into barrel boxes. When I visited Flax Pond Farms in Carver, Massachusetts, I watched modern dry picking. A dry-harvest machine looks something like a giant lawnmower that combs the berries off the vine and into burlap bags. While the machines have replaced the scoops, it is still a backbreaking job.

"Farming is always hard work, regardless," said Dot Angely, who runs the family farm with her husband Jack. In the field, men are bent over, pushing the heavy pickers. Once a bag is full, the berries are dumped by hand into screened boxes to separate the weeds from the fruit. When the picking is complete, a helicopter lifts up stacks of the boxes and delivers them to waiting trucks.

The wet harvest is completely different. In Freetown, Massachusetts, Barbara Araujo runs a small organic bog with her partner David Amaral. On the day of my visit, I arrived just after a sluice gate had released water from an adjacent spring-fed pond to deliver the first shallow flood of about eighteen inches. Dean Petty, an excavator and fellow farmer, plowed his water reel through the bog. The reel is another improbable but useful cranberry harvesting machine that looks like a buggy with a motor on the back atop a series of reels, nicknamed eggbeaters, attached to the front. The reels churn the water just enough to free the berries from the vines without disturbing their roots. Because cranberries have a pocket of air inside, they float and accumulate on the surface.

To finish the process, the bog is flooded again above weed level, and men in waders drag floating booms across the surface of the water to corral the berries. The berries are then funneled into a hopper.

Like many small growers, in order to cultivate cranberries Araujo had to clear the bog, install an irrigation system linked to the nearby pond, and then add enough organic matter and sand to plant the vines. Today, each little berry seems hard won.

All the more reason to let the fruits shine on the table. Slip some into a succulent pork tenderloin before roasting, use them in a maple sweetened sauce for morning pancakes, or freeze them in a bright pink pear and cranberry sorbet. Maybe because I live in a place where they thrive, maybe because their flavor is so unique and the berry is so versatile, or maybe because they are so healthy, cranberries are part of many dishes I love to make all through the year. I hope you dig into these recipes and experiment with some modern ideas beyond cranberry sauce. Don't wait until Thanksgiving!

—Sally Pasley Vargas, Boston, Massachusetts

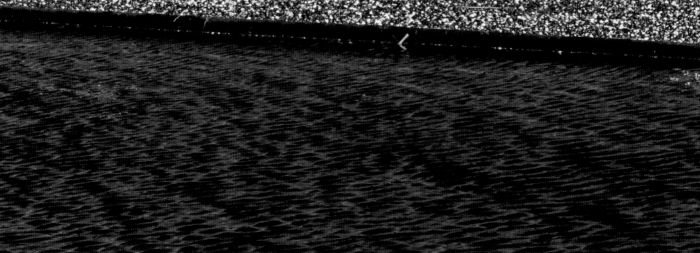

Mornings & Tea Time

Nutty Snack Bars

You could call these breakfast bars or snack bars because they are good any time of day, but they are especially good when you are running out the door on an empty stomach. Take the time to roast the nuts before baking the bars; it makes them extra crunchy. After that, you are on easy street. Warm brown rice syrup with vanilla and salt, stir it into the nuts, and bake. A scant sprinkle of flaky salt on top gives these bars addictive power.

Makes 8 bars

Heat oven to 350°F.

Cut two 9 x 12-inch pieces of parchment. Fit them, perpendicular to each other, into a 9-inch square pan leaving an overhang. Brush or spray with oil.

On a rimmed baking sheet, spread the almonds, cashews, and pumpkin seeds. Bake for 8 minutes, or until fragrant and toasty. Turn oven down to 325°F.

In a bowl, combine the toasted almonds, cashews, pumpkin seeds, brown rice cereal, and cranberries.

In a saucepan over medium heat, stir the syrup, vanilla, and fine salt until warm and fluid. Pour it over the nuts, and mix until well coated. Transfer to the baking pan and spread evenly.

Wet one hand with cold water, and press the mixture to firm and flatten it all the way into the corners of the pan. Sprinkle the coarse salt or sea salt evenly over the top.

Bake for 20 to 25 minutes, or until golden. Set the pan on a wire rack, and cool completely.

Using the parchment, lift the bars in one piece and transfer to a cutting board. With a large, sharp knife, make 1 cut in one direction and 3 cuts in the other to form 8 bars. Wrap each bar separately in waxed paper and store in an airtight container for up to one week.

Olive oil (for the pan)

1 cup raw, whole almonds

¾ cup raw cashews

⅓ cup pumpkin seeds

1 cup puffed brown rice cereal

½ cup dried cranberries

⅓ cup brown rice syrup (available at specialty markets)

2 teaspoons vanilla extract

¼ teaspoon fine sea salt

¼ teaspoon coarse or flaked sea salt

Chocolate Cranberry Zucchini Muffins

These muffins prove that any time of day is a good time for chocolate. Use an ice cream scoop to fill the muffin cups to achieve beautiful rounded tops. Almond flour gives them a rich flavor and moist texture; it is simply finely ground almonds, which you could make yourself in a food processor. To give these muffins sparkle and color, sprinkle them with coarse sugar and a few pinches of chopped pistachios.

Makes 12 muffins

1 cup all-purpose flour

1 cup almond flour

⅓ cup unsweetened Dutch process cocoa powder

1½ teaspoons baking powder

½ teaspoon baking soda

1 teaspoon ground cinnamon

½ teaspoon salt

2 eggs

⅓ cup honey

¼ cup olive oil

¼ cup buttermilk

1 teaspoon vanilla extract

3 cups grated zucchini (3 to 4 medium zucchini)

1 cup fresh or frozen whole cranberries

2 tablespoons coarse sugar, such as turbinado sugar

3 tablespoons chopped green pistachios

Adjust a rack to the middle position of the oven, and heat oven to 400°F.

Generously butter the cups and rims of a standard 12-cup muffin tin, or line the tin with paper cupcake liners. Have on hand a 2½-inch ice-cream scoop.

In a large bowl, whisk together the all-purpose flour, almond flour, cocoa powder, baking powder, baking soda, cinnamon, and salt.

Make a large well in the center of the bowl and break the eggs into it. Add the honey, oil, buttermilk, and vanilla. Beat with a fork to mix thoroughly. With a spatula, stir until the flour is well incorporated. Stir in the zucchini and cranberries.

Using the ice cream scoop, fill each muffin cup, rounded side up, with about ⅓ cup batter.

Sprinkle the muffins with the turbinado sugar and pistachios, and set the tin on a baking sheet. Bake for 23 to 25 minutes, or until a toothpick inserted into the center of a muffin comes out with just a few crumbs.

Set the muffin tin on a rack to cool for 10 minutes. Remove the muffins from the pan and cool on the rack.

Grated zucchini (a vegetable!) has become a popular addition to cakes and muffins to add moisture since the 1960s, also the prime era of the rise of carrot cake, still popular today.

Cornmeal-Cranberry-Pecan Pancakes with Cranberry-Maple Syrup

If you are looking for a New England recipe for a relaxing Sunday breakfast, leave the pancake mix at the back of the cupboard and take a little extra time to make these. Start by gently poaching the cranberries in maple syrup and then leave them to steep and cool. The syrup tames the sour berries and yields a lovely ruby syrup to serve with the pancakes. You can make the syrup ahead of time and refrigerate it with the berries for up to two weeks.

Makes 14-16 pancakes

FOR THE CRANBERRY-MAPLE SYRUP

1½ cups fresh or frozen cranberries

¾ cup maple syrup

3 tablespoons apple juice

1 teaspoon vanilla extract

FOR THE PANCAKES

1 cup yellow cornmeal

1 teaspoon salt

1 cup boiling water

1 cup milk

2 eggs

3 tablespoons honey

1 teaspoon vanilla extract

3 tablespoons butter, melted

1 cup flour

2 teaspoons baking powder

Maple steeped cranberries (above)

½ cup pecans, coarsely chopped

Vegetable oil (for the skillet)

For the Cranberry-Maple Syrup:
In a small saucepan over medium heat, bring the cranberries, syrup, and apple juice to a boil. Adjust the heat to simmer and cook for 3 minutes. Remove from heat, cover the pan, and let the cranberries steep for 15 minutes. Stir in the vanilla.

Pour the syrup into a shallow dish and place in the freezer for 20 minutes, or chill in the refrigerator until cool. (You can make this up to two weeks in advance.)

Set a strainer over a bowl and drain the cranberries, reserving the liquid. Use the berries in the pancakes, and reserve the syrup to pour over them.

For the Pancakes:
In a large bowl, stir the cornmeal, salt, and boiling water together. Let stand for 10 minutes.

In a small bowl, whisk the milk, eggs, honey, vanilla, and melted butter until combined. Pour over the cornmeal. Add the flour and baking powder to the bowl, and stir with a sturdy whisk until the batter is smooth. Stir in the strained cranberries and the pecans.

Set a pancake griddle or large, seasoned skillet over medium heat. Spread about 1 teaspoon vegetable oil in the pan, and wipe out the excess with a paper towel. When the pan is hot, drop the batter by ⅓ cupfuls into the skillet. Cook for 2 to 3 minutes, or until the pancakes bubble on top and the bottoms are browned. Turn them over and cook for 2 minutes more, or until golden brown. Repeat with the remaining batter, adding more oil to the pan as necessary. If batter thickens as it sits, stir in a little more milk to return it to the desired consistency.

Serve with the cranberry syrup.

Crunchy Vanilla Almond Granola

This granola surpasses any you can buy ready-made, and puts the crunch back into crunchy granola. It takes about 25 minutes to make, and only 5 minutes are hands on, so baking it has become routine in our house. It has just a hint of salt, enough to make it addictive, and is very lightly sweetened. You can start your morning off without sugar shock. Dried cranberries add the perfect counterpoint, and give another health boost to the most important meal of the day.

Makes about 8 cups

Heat oven to 350°F. Line a rimmed baking sheet with parchment paper about 1 inch larger all around than the size of the pan.

In a large bowl, combine the oats, almonds, flax seeds, and pumpkin seeds.

In a saucepan over medium heat, stir the honey, olive oil, vanilla, and salt for 2 minutes, or until warm and fluid, and the salt dissolves. Pour it over the oats, and stir to coat them. Spread on the baking sheet.

Bake for 15 minutes, then remove the pan from the oven. Grasp each corner of the parchment and pull it toward the center to mound the granola into a pile. Stir with a large spoon and spread it out again in one layer. Return it to the oven for 5 minutes. Remove, and mound the granola in the center again. If it still looks pale in places, stir, spread, and return the pan to the oven to toast for 3 or 4 minutes more. (Total baking time is 20 to 25 minutes.) Leave on the baking sheet to cool.

Transfer to a bowl and stir in the cranberries. Leave to cool completely. Store in an airtight jar or tin for up to 2 weeks.

5 cups old-fashioned rolled oats (not instant)

1 cup whole almonds

⅔ cup flax seeds

⅔ cup pumpkin seeds

½ cup honey

¼ cup olive oil

1 tablespoon vanilla extract

½ teaspoon salt

1 cup dried cranberries

Cranberry-Apricot Cream Scones

One summer, years ago, my four-year old son and I traveled with my husband on business to England where we stayed at a fancy manor hotel. It was early June, and strawberries were at their peak. With time on our hands, my son and I whiled away an afternoon with tea and scones, served with a heaping plate of strawberries and clotted cream. As though he were repeating lines in a script, my son asked in all innocence, "Please sir, may I have some more?" We were promptly supplied with more of everything and after some negotiations with the chef, I obtained this recipe, which I have adapted to family-size servings. Don't think you're being cheeky if you ask for more; after all, it was perfectly acceptable at the manor house.

Makes 1 dozen

Set an oven rack in the middle position, and heat oven to 425°F. Line a baking sheet with parchment paper.

In a bowl, whisk the egg, vanilla, and 1 cup of the cream.

In the bowl of an electric mixer fitted with the paddle attachment, combine the all-purpose flour, cake flour, 3 tablespoons sugar, baking powder, salt, and orange zest. Add the butter slices and mix on medium-low speed until the butter is in pea-size pieces. (You can also do this by hand with your fingertips.)

Remove the bowl from the stand and add the apricots. With your hands, toss to separate them and coat them in the flour. Repeat with the cranberries. Add the egg and cream mixture, and stir with a spatula until the flour is incorporated.

Scrape the dough onto a generously floured work surface and knead a few times, just until the dough comes together. Do not overwork it. It should be soft but not too sticky. Roll the dough to a ¾-inch thickness. Dip a 3-inch round cutter in flour and press it straight down into the dough without twisting. Repeat until all the dough is used, dipping the cutter in flour between cuts. Gather the scraps, knead once or twice, and roll and cut out scones again until all the dough is used. Transfer the rounds to the baking sheet.

With a pastry brush, brush scones with the remaining cream. Place them in the oven and immediately decrease the heat to 400°F. Bake for 20 to 25 minutes, or until the scones are lightly browned. Cool on the sheet for 10 minutes. Sprinkle with confectioners' sugar and serve.

Note: To keep scones from rising unevenly, press the cutter straight down into dough without twisting it.

1 egg

½ teaspoon vanilla extract

1 cup plus 2 tablespoons heavy cream

2 cups all-purpose flour, plus more for rolling

1 cup cake flour

3 tablespoons granulated sugar, plus 1 tablespoon for the whipped cream

4 teaspoons baking powder

½ teaspoon salt

1 tablespoon finely grated orange zest

10 tablespoons (1¼ sticks) cold, unsalted butter, thinly sliced

⅓ cup (3 ounces) dried apricots, cut into small dice

1 cup fresh or frozen cranberries, coarsely chopped

Confectioners' sugar (for the baked scones)

Cranberry-Chocolate Babka

I lived in Indiana for years and I often flew to visit my family in New Jersey. A friend and die-hard New Yorker always insisted I stop in the city to pick up a babka from The Babka Bakery on the Upper West Side to take home to the Midwest. I would do that until somewhere along the way I came up with a recipe to save myself the long trip. A good thing, too, since the bakery has closed. This is my latest version. I love the contrast of the tart cranberries and the chocolate. Yes, it's a bit of a project, but a fun one. After you try it once, you will want to make it again for special occasions. You can also double the recipe, bake the loaves, and freeze one for another day.

Makes 1 loaf

FOR THE DOUGH

2 cups all-purpose flour

1 packet instant yeast*

½ teaspoon salt

⅓ cup milk

1 whole egg

1 egg yolk

½ stick (2 ounces) unsalted butter, softened at room temperature

1 teaspoon vegetable oil (for the rising bowl)

FOR THE FILLING

1½ cups whole fresh or frozen cranberries

½ cup granulated sugar

2 tablespoons orange juice

1 teaspoon finely grated orange zest

In an electric mixer fitted with the paddle attachment, stir 1½ cups flour with the yeast and the salt. Add the milk, whole egg, egg yolk, and butter. Beat on medium speed for 4 minutes, or until very sticky and stretchy.

Add the remaining ½ cup flour and mix for 2 minutes more. The dough will be soft. With a rubber spatula, scrape down the sides of the bowl and form the dough into a ball. (Wet your hands if the dough is very sticky.)

Sprinkle a clean bowl with the oil. Place the dough in the bowl and turn it to coat it all over with oil. Cover the bowl with plastic wrap and let the dough rise for 1 to 1½ hours, or until doubled in bulk.

In a small saucepan over medium heat, bring the cranberries, sugar, orange juice, and orange zest to a boil. Lower the heat and simmer for 5 to 6 minutes, or until the cranberries are soft. Remove from heat and cool slightly.

In a food processor, pulse the cranberry mixture 3 or 4 times, or until it is coarsely pureed with a few visible chunks of cranberry. Scrape into a bowl and refrigerate until cold.

In food processor, pulse the walnuts, sugar, flour, cocoa, cinnamon, salt, and butter until it is crumbly and dark brown. Transfer to a bowl. Set aside ¼ cup of the streusel for the loaf pan.

Generously butter a 9 x 5-inch loaf pan. Sprinkle with ¼ cup of the reserved streusel, tilting the pan to cover the bottom and sides.

On a lightly floured surface, roll the dough into a 14-inch square. With a pastry brush dipped in water, brush a 1-inch border on all four sides. Spread the cranberry filling on the dough to the edge of the border. Spread the remaining streusel on the cranberries. With a rolling pin, gently press the streusel into the dough.

FOR THE STREUSEL

⅓ cup walnuts

¼ cup brown sugar

⅔ cup flour

2 tablespoons Dutch process unsweetened cocoa powder

2 teaspoons ground cinnamon

⅛ teaspoon salt

3 tablespoons unsalted butter, cut into slices

TO SHAPE AND BAKE THE BABKA

Butter (for the loaf pan)

Extra flour (for rolling)

1 egg, beaten with 1 tablespoon water

Instant yeast, also packaged as rapid rise yeast, is a slightly different strain of yeast than regular active dried yeast. Instant yeast is dried and milled into smaller particles than its original cousin and its main advantage is that it does not have to be dissolved in water and "proofed" before using.

Starting at a long edge nearest you, roll the dough into a tight cylinder. With your fingers, pinch the long seam together and turn the roll so the seam side is down.

With a serrated knife, cut across the log in the center to make 2 rolls. Pinch the ends together and roll each one back and forth gently to stretch it to about 12 inches. Set it horizontally on the work surface.

Place the second roll vertically on top of the first to form a cross. Pick up the left arm of the cross and twist it over and to the right of the center roll. Pick up the right arm of the cross and twist it over and to the left of the center roll. You should now have a loaf with three bumps.

Tuck the ends under the loaf and set it in the pan. Cover loosely with plastic wrap and leave in warm place to rise for 1 hour, or until the loaf is about 1 inch above the top of the pan.

Set a rack in the middle position and heat oven to 350°F. Place the loaf pan on a baking sheet.

Bake for 40 to 45 minutes, or until an instant read thermometer registers 190°F when inserted into the center of the loaf. (Total baking time is about 1 hour.) Check after 35 minutes and if the loaf is browning too quickly, place a piece of foil loosely over the top.

Set the loaf on a rack and cool for 10 minutes. Turn the loaf out of the pan onto a wire rack to cool. To serve, cut in thick slices.

Cranberry-Maple Butter

Don't let any extra syrup or cranberries go to waste! Make as little or as much of this flavored butter as you like (recipe can be doubled or tripled). Then spread it on biscuits, toast, or even French toast for a special morning treat.

Makes ½ cup

Scoop out the cranberries from the syrup and coarsely chop them. Return them to the syrup.

In a small bowl, beat the butter, cranberries and syrup, salt, and orange zest until fluffy. Pack the butter into a ramekin, or form into a 4-inch log on a piece of parchment paper. Twist the ends of the parchment paper and roll the mixture back and forth a few times to form a round log. Refrigerate until ready to use.

¼ cup cranberries steeped in maple syrup

4 ounces (1 stick) unsalted butter, at room temperature

Pinch of salt

½ teaspoon finely grated orange zest

Tasty Little Bites

Squash, Blue Cheese, and Cranberry Tart

Roasted sweet squash, creamy ricotta, salty blue cheese, and cranberries complement each other beautifully in this tart, which can go with a bowl of soup or a cocktail. Store-bought puff pastry takes the heavy lifting out of the recipe, but it should be made with butter. Other kinds of puff pastry aren't as good.

Serves 10-12

Heat oven to 450°F. Have 3 baking sheets on hand.

On one baking sheet, mound the squash in the center. Drizzle with vegetable oil, and sprinkle with rosemary and sage. With your hands, toss to coat the cubes thoroughly. Spread in one layer and sprinkle with salt and pepper. Roast for 20 minutes, or until tender and golden.

Decrease oven temperature to 400°F. Line the other 2 baking sheets with parchment paper.

On a lightly floured surface, unfold the dough and discard the inner papers. Dust the top with flour, and roll it gently, just enough to flatten it evenly. Cut it into 2 rectangles that are about 6 inches wide by 15 inches long. Transfer each to a baking sheet.

With a pizza cutter or sharp knife, trim all four edges to make them even. Gently press a fork along each of the long sides of the dough to make a ¼-inch border. Spread half the ricotta down the center of each tart, leaving a ½-inch border. On each tart, distribute half the blue cheese over the ricotta, and top with half the squash.

Transfer to the oven and bake for 15 minutes.

Remove the tarts from the oven and distribute half the cranberries over each. Return to the oven and continue baking for 10 to 12 minutes, or until the pastry is golden and the cranberries are soft. Remove and sprinkle with more rosemary and sage. Cut into rectangles or wedges, and serve warm.

Vegetable oil (for the baking sheet)

1 peeled butternut squash half (about 1¼ pounds), cut into ¾-inch cubes

1 tablespoon chopped fresh rosemary, plus more for garnish

1 tablespoon chopped fresh sage, plus more for garnish

Salt and pepper, to taste

Flour (for rolling)

1 pound all-butter frozen puff pastry (store-bought), defrosted

1 cup whole-milk ricotta

3 ounces blue cheese, cut into thin slices

⅔ cup fresh or frozen cranberries

Scottish Oatcakes with Dried Cranberries

I confess, I have a weakness for crackers. Good Scottish oatcakes, a crisp-bread popular in the northern cold, wet climate of that country, are hard to come by unless you make them yourself. These rounds with sweet dried cranberries deliver a lot of flavor. Enjoy with a glass of wine, or with a spoonful of jam and a cup of tea.

Makes 2 dozen oatcakes

1½ cups old-fashioned rolled oats

½ cup all-purpose flour

½ cup whole-wheat flour

2 tablespoons brown sugar

1 teaspoon baking powder

¼ teaspoon salt

10 tablespoons (1¼ sticks) cold, unsalted butter, cut into thin slices

5 tablespoons milk, plus more as needed

½ cup dried cranberries

Flour (for forming the oatcakes)

Heat oven to 350°F. Line 2 baking sheets with parchment paper.

In a food processor, pulse the oats, all-purpose flour, whole-wheat flour, brown sugar, baking powder, salt, and butter until well mixed. Add the milk and pulse until the mixture begins to clump together. If the dough seems dry, add more milk, 1 tablespoon at a time. Add the cranberries and pulse 2 or 3 times to mix them into the dough.

Turn the dough out onto a lightly floured work surface. Knead briefly, and form it into 2 even logs. Cut each log into twelve even pieces. Roll the pieces into balls and place them on the baking sheets, 12 per sheet. With the palm of your hand, flatten the balls. Sprinkle them lightly with flour.

Place about ½ cup flour on a small plate. Using a flat-bottomed glass or dry measuring cup, press hard on the oatcakes to flatten them until they are about 3 inches wide, dipping the glass in the flour as needed to keep it from sticking to the oatcakes.

Bake for 20 to 25 minutes, or until golden brown on the bottom. Transfer to a rack to cool. Store in an airtight tin for up to 1 week.

Cranberry Peach Salsa

While late-season peaches and early fresh cranberries may only appear in the market during a tiny window of time, celebrate them when they do. There are plenty of reasons to make this salsa. If the peaches are ripe and the fresh crop of cranberries hasn't come in yet, use frozen cranberries. Once peach season has passed, rely on mangoes for that sweet and juicy element. I don't bother to peel the peaches. The faint bitter edge of the cranberries combined with lush and juicy peaches, lime juice, a feisty pepper, and a good handful of cilantro make this a winning complement to tortilla chips and your favorite grilled chicken. Poblanos are typically fairly mild, with just enough heat to add some pleasant spice to the salsa.

Makes 3 cups

In a saucepan over medium heat, bring the cranberries, sugar, and orange juice to a boil. Lower the heat and simmer for 5 minutes, or until the cranberries soften but have not fallen apart. Transfer to a bowl to allow to cool.

In a strainer set over a bowl, drain the cranberries. Reserve the cranberry syrup for another use, such as cranberry lime rickey (see page 109) or other drinks.

In another bowl, stir together the drained cranberries, peaches, poblano, onion, lime juice, salt, pepper, and cilantro. Chill until ready to serve.

Serve with chips and beer, with roast chicken, or in a taco with just about any leftover you choose.

1 cup fresh or frozen cranberries

¼ cup sugar

Juice of ½ large orange

2 medium peaches, cut into small dice

½ poblano pepper, seeded and cut into small dice

2 tablespoons finely diced red onion

Juice of 2 limes

Salt and pepper, to taste

½ cup packed cilantro leaves, coarsely chopped

Tortilla chips (for serving)

How to Make Tortilla Chips in the Oven

Consider these instructions as guidelines, using 6 tortillas as an example. Make as many or as few as you like. My apologies in advance. You won't be able to stop eating them.

Heat oven to 400°F. Brush 6 corn tortillas lightly with olive oil (you will use about 1 tablespoon for 6 tortillas). Stack them and cut them into 6 wedges. Spread them on a baking sheet and bake for 10 to 12 minutes, or until golden. Sprinkle with salt.

Danish Sandwiches (*Smorrebrod*)

Let me introduce you to the best thing since sliced bread: Danish *smorrebrod* (from the word butter [*smor*] and bread [*brod*], and pronounced *smuhr-broht*). These open-faced sandwiches invite all kinds of improvisations. You can't beat them as appetizers or party fare. Pickled cranberries add a compelling twist when paired with smoked salmon, crunchy cucumber, radishes, and micro greens. But don't rule out ham and Dijon mustard, or roast beef and horseradish, or any combination that appeals to you. I buy dense whole meal rye bread made with crushed rye kernels, rye flour, and other grains. Sometimes called "fitness bread," the brick-shaped loaf comes sliced, available at specialty markets.

Serves 4

6 tablespoons unsalted butter, at room temperature

2 tablespoons prepared white horseradish

1 teaspoon finely grated lemon zest

Salt and pepper, to taste

4 slices dense rye bread

6 ounces sliced smoked salmon

Juice of ½ lemon

½ English cucumber, thinly sliced

8 radishes, thinly sliced

4 ounces micro greens

1 cup pickled cranberries
(see page 69)

In a small bowl, mash together the butter, horseradish, lemon zest, salt, and pepper.

On a cutting board, spread out the bread and slather each slice with ¼ of the butter. Divide the salmon among the 4 slices, and sprinkle with lemon juice. Top with cucumber slices, radishes, and micro greens. Distribute the cranberries on top. Slice each piece of bread into 4 triangles and serve.

Did You Know?

Health benefits of cranberries include reducing the risk of cardiovascular disease, helping slow down tumor progression, and lowering the risk of urinary tract infections.

Roasted Harvest Vegetable Soup with Cranberry Coulis

At the end of summer before there is even a nip in the air, markets fill with mountains of squash and root vegetables that beg to go into soup. Think of this recipe as a guideline, and pick and choose what is available to you. This large batch is suitable for serving a crowd, or for stashing some away in the freezer to pull out on a rainy night. Moroccan spices add a touch of warmth to the colorful little specks of vegetables.

Roast the vegetables until tender but still a little firm. Before pureeing, baste them in the toasted spice and butter mixture, add water, and cook just long enough to bring the flavors together. The soup will be thick when pureed, so add enough water to bring it to a soupy consistency. A spoonful of yogurt adds a cooling element, while cranberries offer a tart and sweet accent.

Serves 10

In a small saucepan over medium heat, stir together the cranberries, wine, sugar, bay leaf, ginger, and salt. Bring to a boil. Lower the heat, and simmer for 7 minutes, or until the cranberries are soft. Cool to room temperature.

Remove the bay leaf and ginger. In a blender, puree the mixture until smooth.

Heat oven to 450°F. Lightly oil 2 rimmed baking sheets.

On the baking sheets, spread the onion, carrots, celery, parsnips, turnip, and squash. Drizzle with the oil. With your hands, toss together, massaging the oil into the vegetables. Spread in one layer. Sprinkle with salt and pepper. Roast for 25 to 30 minutes, or until tender but still slightly firm when pierced with the tip of a paring knife.

In a soup pot over medium heat, melt the butter. Add the *ras el hanout* and cook, stirring for 30 seconds to toast the spices. Add the vegetables to the pot and stir to coat them with the spice. Add enough water to cover the vegetables. Over medium heat, bring to a boil. Decrease the heat to a simmer, and continue to cook for 5 minutes. Cool briefly.

In a food processor, working in batches, puree the vegetables and broth until coarse and a little chunky. Transfer to a clean pot. Add the lemon juice and honey. Cook, stirring until the mixture comes to a boil. Thin with more water if the soup is thick. Taste for seasoning and add more salt and pepper, if you like.

Garnish with spoonfuls of yogurt and drizzle with cranberry coulis.

FOR THE CRANBERRY COULIS

1½ cups fresh or frozen cranberries

¾ cup white wine

⅓ cup sugar

1 bay leaf

2 (⅛-inch thick) slices fresh ginger

Pinch of salt

FOR THE SOUP

Vegetable oil (for the baking sheet)

1 large onion, cut into six wedges

1 pound unpeeled carrots (3–4 large), ends trimmed and cut into 1½-inch lengths

2 stalks celery, cut into 1½-inch pieces

6 small parsnips (12 ounces), ends trimmed and cut into 1½-inch lengths

1 large white turnip (12 ounces), peeled and cut into 1½-inch chunks

½ peeled butternut squash (about 1 pound), cut into 1½-inch chunks

3 tablespoons olive oil

Salt and pepper, to taste

3 tablespoons butter

2 tablespoons ras el hanout

6–8 cups water

2 tablespoons lemon juice

2 tablespoons honey

1 cup plain yogurt (for garnish)

Salads & Vegetables

Roasted Carrots and Cranberries

It's fun to transform everyday vegetables such as carrots into something special with just a few spices. Here roasted carrots are seasoned with crushed coriander, cumin, and fresh ginger to take them to a whole new level with roasted cranberries and mint. Parsnips, turnips, celery root, even radishes, could go into the mix if you want to make a bonanza of hearty vegetables.

Serves 4

Olive oil (for sprinkling)

1 tablespoon finely chopped fresh ginger

1 tablespoon coarsely crushed coriander seed

2 teaspoons coarsely crushed cumin seed

1½ pounds slender carrots, trimmed and peeled

2–3 tablespoons olive oil

Salt and pepper, to taste

1 cup fresh or frozen cranberries

2 tablespoon unsalted butter, cut into slices

1 tablespoon honey

2–3 sprigs fresh mint, leaves torn into pieces (for garnish)

Aleppo pepper or crushed red pepper (for garnish)

Heat oven to 425°F. Oil a rimmed baking sheet and an 8-inch square glass or ceramic baking dish.

In a small bowl, stir together the ginger, coriander seed, and cumin seed.

On the baking sheet, spread the carrots. Drizzle with 2 tablespoons of the oil. With your hands, massage the oil into the carrots so they are well coated. Sprinkle with salt, pepper, and the spice mixture. Roast for 20 to 25 minutes, or until tender and golden.

Meanwhile, in the baking dish spread the cranberries in one layer. Drizzle them with 1 teaspoon of the oil, and toss to coat them. Sprinkle with salt and pepper, and roast for 5 minutes, or until cranberries soften slightly but still hold their shape. With a slotted spoon, transfer the cranberries to a small bowl.

Add the butter and honey to the cranberry juices in the baking dish. Stir to melt the butter. (Pop the dish back in the oven for a half a minute if the butter doesn't melt.)

Scatter the roasted cranberries over the carrots on the baking sheet. Drizzle with the honey butter, and sprinkle with the mint and Aleppo or red pepper.

Cauliflower Biryani

Cauliflower that is finely chopped in a food processor looks like rice, which satisfies anyone who wants to cut out starchy carbohydrates but still misses them. Maybe you're not really fooling anyone, but this is worth making anyway. Warm spices such as turmeric, cumin, and coriander infuse the cauliflower rice with a lot of flavor. Add cooked French lentils, cranberries, toasted pistachios, and fresh herbs, and you end up with a dish good enough to eat by itself for lunch or to serve beside lamb chops or chicken. I like to roast the cauliflower in the oven, spread on a baking sheet. It's a bit less messy than sautéing on top of the stove, and the resulting texture is light and fluffy.

Serves 6

Heat oven to 350°F. Have on hand a small baking dish. Line a rimmed baking sheet with parchment paper.

In a small saucepan over medium heat, bring the lentils, water, and salt to a boil. Lower the heat and simmer for 18 to 20 minutes, or until tender. Drain in a colander.

In the baking dish, spread the pistachios. Toast in the oven for 6 to 7 minutes, turning often, or until toasted. Cool.

Turn oven temperature up to 400°F.

In a food processor, pulse half the cauliflower until finely chopped. Transfer to the baking sheet and pulse the remaining cauliflower. Mound it in the center of the baking sheet. Drizzle with the olive oil. Sprinkle with the salt, turmeric, coriander, and cumin. Toss with your hands to mix together evenly. Spread in one layer, and bake for 7 minutes.

Remove from the oven, stir, and spread again on the sheet. Bake for an additional 7 minutes (total cooking time is 14 minutes.) Transfer to a serving bowl. Stir in the lemon juice, cooked lentils, pistachios, cranberries, carrot, parsley, and mint. Taste for seasoning and add more salt and lemon juice, if you like.

½ cup Le Puy or other small, dark French lentils

1½ cups water

⅛ teaspoon salt

½ cup unsalted green pistachios

1 head cauliflower, quartered, cored, and sliced

2 tablespoons olive oil

½ teaspoon salt

2 teaspoons ground turmeric

1 teaspoon coriander seed, crushed in a mortar

½ teaspoon ground cumin

3 tablespoons lemon juice

½ cup dried cranberries

1 carrot, peeled and grated

2 tablespoons chopped fresh parsley

2 tablespoons chopped fresh mint

Sautéed Kale with Cranberries and Pine Nuts

The sweetness of dried cranberries and a splash of cider offset the earthy, faintly bitter, flavor of kale. Choose dinosaur (lacinato) or curly kale; both work well in this stir fry.

Serves 6

Heat oven to 350°F.

On a small baking sheet, spread the pine nuts. Bake for 7 to 8 minutes, or until golden.

In a large Dutch oven, heat the oil and garlic over medium heat until the garlic sizzles and turns pale golden. Add the cranberries and cider. Stir for 30 seconds, or until the cranberries start to soften.

Add as many handfuls of kale as will fit in the pot. Add salt and pepper to taste. Cook and turn with tongs until the kale begins to wilt. As the volume decreases, add more raw kale to the pan, until all the kale has been added. Cook for 5 minutes, or until tender. If the pan seems dry, add water 1 tablespoon at a time. Stir in the lemon juice and pine nuts. Taste and add more salt and pepper, if you like. Sprinkle with lemon zest.

½ cup pine nuts

2 tablespoons olive oil

2 clove garlics, thinly sliced

⅓ cup dried cranberries

⅓ cup apple cider

2 large bunches kale, stemmed and torn into 2-inch pieces

Salt and pepper, to taste

1 tablespoon lemon juice

Finely grated zest of ½ lemon

Did you know?

Cranberries bounce! They float, too, because of a tiny pocket of air inside each berry. For that reason, bogs can be flooded during harvest and the floating berries are collected with the help of "eggbeaters," reels that churn the water and loosen the berries from the vine.

Colorful Salad with Clementines, Goat Cheese, and Dried Cranberries

Salty, soft cheese plays against juicy sweet clementines, peppery greens, and slightly bitter radicchio in this salad. The concentrated sweetness of dried cranberries and crisp toasted nuts add two other levels of texture and flavor. The surprise element is the mint. Although I often make some version of this salad from the fall to early spring to take advantage of colorful citrus fruits as they come into season, it has a place on the summer table, too, with stone fruits like peaches and plums. Citrus dressing carries the sweet theme without being cloying, and ties all the individual components together.

Serves 4

FOR THE DRESSING

3 tablespoons orange juice

1 tablespoon lemon juice

2 teaspoons sherry vinegar

½ teaspoon honey

½ teaspoon crushed coriander seed

Salt and pepper, to taste

6 tablespoons olive oil

FOR THE SALAD

½ cup walnuts

4 clementines

4 handfuls dark greens such as arugula, baby spinach, baby kale, or watercress

1 handful fresh mint leaves

½ small head radicchio, leaves torn into large pieces

4 radishes, thinly sliced

½ cup dried cranberries

4 ounces goat cheese, cut into rounds

In a bowl, whisk the orange juice, lemon juice, vinegar, honey, coriander, salt, and pepper.

Gradually whisk in the oil. Taste for seasoning, and add more salt and pepper, if you like.

Heat oven to 350°F.

On a baking sheet, spread the walnuts. Toast for 8 minutes, or until aromatic. Cool.

With a sharp paring knife, trim the ends of each clementine. Stand one fruit on a cutting board with a flat end down. Use a sawing motion, curving with the shape of the orange to cut the pith and peel from top to bottom. Repeat all around the clementine until it is peeled. Cut into rounds. Repeat with the remaining clementines.

In a salad bowl, combine the salad greens, mint leaves, radicchio, radishes, cranberries, and clementines. Toss with dressing, to taste. Top with the goat cheese rounds, and sprinkle with the walnuts.

Lentil, Arugula, and Feta Salad

Small green lentils have a slight peppery flavor and stay intact when cooked, making them ideal for a hearty salad. Arugula and crushed coriander carry the pungent theme forward, and contrast with salty feta, pickled onions, and sweet cranberries. If you don't have a mortar, enclose the whole coriander in a zip lock bag and crush them with a rolling pin.

Serves 4

In a small bowl, whisk together the vinegar, salt, pepper, and coriander seed.

Gradually whisk in the oil. Taste for seasoning, and add more salt and pepper, if you like.

Heat oven to 350°F.

Bring a saucepan of salted water to a boil. Add the lentils, return to a boil and lower the heat. Simmer for 18 to 20 minutes, or until they are tender but still hold their shape. Drain into a large strainer and transfer to a bowl. Stir in 1 tablespoon of the oil and 1 tablespoon of the vinegar. Add pepper and more salt, if you like. Cool.

In the center of a baking sheet, mound the onions. Sprinkle with the remaining 1 tablespoon of oil, the remaining 1 tablespoon of vinegar, sugar, salt, and pepper. Toss and spread out on the sheet. Bake for 10 minutes or until soft but not brown. Cool.

In a salad bowl, toss the arugula with the vinaigrette. Add the lentils, onions, feta, and cranberries.

FOR THE DRESSING

1 tablespoon sherry vinegar

Salt and pepper, to taste

1 teaspoon coriander seed, coarsely crushed in a mortar

3 tablespoons olive oil

FOR THE SALAD

1 cup small green lentils, such as Le Puy

2 tablespoons olive oil

2 tablespoons sherry vinegar

Salt and pepper, to taste

1 red onion, halved and thinly sliced

¼ teaspoon sugar

¼ red onion, thinly sliced

2 bunches (6 cups) arugula

3 ounces feta cheese, crumbled

½ cup dried cranberries

Shaved Brussels Sprouts with Apples, Walnuts, and Cranberries

By mid-winter, we need strong flavors to snap the taste buds to attention, and these thinly sliced raw Brussels sprouts dressed with lemon and mustard do just that. To shave the sprouts, you need a mandolin or other hand-held slicer, a food processor with a slicing blade, or a thin, sharp knife and plenty of patience. Toasted walnuts on top add richness and crunch.

Serves 4

½ cup walnuts

3 tablespoons lemon juice

4 teaspoons Dijon mustard

Salt and pepper, to taste

3 tablespoons walnut oil or olive oil

1 pound large Brussels sprouts, discolored and loose outer leaves removed

1 apple, cut into thin julienne strips

½ cup dried cranberries

Set oven at 350°F.

On a baking sheet, spread the walnuts. Toast for 8 minutes, or until aromatic and crisp.

In a bowl large enough to hold the salad, whisk together the lemon juice, mustard, salt, and pepper. Gradually whisk in the oil.

Using a mandolin or another slicer, grip a stem end of a sprout with your fingers and slice the round until the sprout is too short to safely slice. Continue with the remaining sprouts. (To use the slicing blade of a food processor, trim and discard the stems first.) Transfer to the bowl of dressing.

Add the apples and cranberries. Toss to coat the salad with dressing. Taste for seasoning, and add more salt and pepper, if you like.

Transfer the salad to a serving bowl and sprinkle with toasted walnuts.

Toasted Quinoa with Butternut Squash, Dried Cranberries, and Pumpkin Seeds

Grains and vegetables in a bowl have caught on as a satisfying meal-in-one. Here, swap out any grain for the quinoa: red rice, brown rice, or even a mix of red and white quinoa and buckwheat. Toasting the grains for a few minutes before cooking adds another nice dimension. This is a perfect meal to enjoy when you want something both simple and comforting.

Serves 4

Heat oven to 450°F. Lightly oil a rimmed baking sheet.

Mound the squash in the center of the baking sheet. Drizzle with 1 tablespoon of the oil. With your hands, toss to coat the squash in the oil. Spread in one layer and sprinkle with the chili powder, salt, and pepper. Bake for 15 minutes, or until the squash is tender and lightly browned.

In a dry saucepan over medium-high heat, stir the quinoa constantly for about 3 minutes, or until golden brown and fragrant. Add a pinch of salt and the water (it will sputter) and bring to a boil. Lower the heat, add the onions, and cover the pot. Simmer for 15 minutes, or until the water is absorbed.

Remove the pot from the heat and sprinkle the cranberries over the top of the quinoa. Add the spinach and cover the pot. Let rest for 10 minutes.

Meanwhile, in a skillet, heat 1 teaspoon of the oil over medium heat. Add the pumpkin seeds. Stir and shake the pan for about 3 minutes, or until the pumpkin seeds turn from green to olive to lightly golden brown. Sprinkle with a pinch of salt and transfer to a plate.

With a fork, fluff up the quinoa and mix with the cranberries and spinach. Taste for seasoning, and add salt and pepper if you like. Serve in bowls, sprinkled with the toasted pumpkin seeds.

Vegetable oil (for the baking sheet)

½ peeled butternut squash (about 1 pound), cut into ¾-inch cubes

1 tablespoon plus 1 teaspoon olive oil

¾ teaspoon ancho chili powder

Salt and pepper, to taste

1 cup quinoa

2 cups water

½ red onion, finely diced

½ cup dried cranberries

2 large handfuls baby spinach (about 2½ ounces)

⅓ cup pumpkin seeds

Savory Entrees

Brisket with Cranberries

Chilly days call for warm and cozy gatherings with family and friends. They will be well fed and happy with this slow-cooked brisket, a bowl of mashed potatoes, and a salad. The cook will be happy too. After a few minutes of browning, the meat goes into the oven for the afternoon; it will be ready to slice and serve when you are ready to eat. It is even better a day later after resting in the fridge overnight. If you are lucky enough to have leftovers, they make terrific sandwiches on soft rolls, or shred the meat and toss into pasta with some of the sauce.

Serves 6

1 (3½- to 4-pound) flat-cut brisket

Salt and pepper, to taste

2 tablespoons olive oil

3 cloves garlic, finely chopped

2 large onions, halved and sliced

½ cup sherry vinegar

½ cup brown sugar

½ cup canned crushed tomatoes

3 cups (12 ounces) fresh or frozen cranberries

3 cups chicken stock

2 tablespoons chopped parsley (for garnish)

Heat oven to 325°F. Sprinkle the brisket on both sides with salt and pepper.

In a large pot with a lid, heat the oil over medium-high heat. Add the brisket and brown for 4 to 5 minutes on a side. Transfer to a platter.

Add the garlic and onions to the pot and cook, stirring occasionally, for 5 minutes.

Stir in the vinegar, brown sugar, tomatoes, cranberries, and stock. Bring to a boil. Return the brisket to the pot, cover, and transfer to the oven. Cook for 3½ hours. Remove the lid and continue cooking for 30 more minutes, or until the meat is tender but not falling apart.

Transfer the meat to a cutting board. Cover loosely with foil and let rest for 20 minutes.

Set a strainer over a bowl. A few ladles at a time, strain the sauce, pressing the sides of the strainer with a rubber spatula until the pulp is almost dry. Discard the pulp. If necessary, skim the fat from the sauce.

Slice the brisket and set it on a platter. Spoon some sauce over the top, and sprinkle with parsley. Serve with more sauce on the side.

Duck Breast with Caramelized Apples and Cranberries

To cook a whole duck feels like a "project," but sautéing a duck breast can be accomplished in half an hour. The breast, called *magret* produces almost steak-like red, juicy meat. In fact, this simple preparation is much like that of steak except the duck is seared on the fat side over low heat, so that the fat slowly renders as the skin crisps and browns before slipping the skillet into the oven until the meat reaches the desired temperature.

Serves 4

In a non-stick skillet over medium heat, melt the butter. Add the sugar and apples. Cook, swirling the pan from time to time, for about 3 minutes, or until the apples brown on one side. With tongs, carefully turn them and cook for 2 minutes more, or until they are golden and caramelized. Stir in the lemon juice. Set aside in a warm place while you cook the duck.

Heat oven to 350°F. Have on hand a large, heavy skillet with heatproof handles. Pat the breasts dry with a paper towel. Use a sharp knife to score the skin of each breast in a diagonal crosshatch pattern of cuts about ¾ inches apart. Sprinkle them generously on both sides with salt and pepper.

Set the skillet on medium-low heat, and heat for about 2 minutes, or until hot. Place the duck, skin side down, in the skillet. Cook for 10 minutes, or until the skin browns. When an abundance of rendered fat accumulates in the pan, temporarily transfer the duck to a plate and spoon off and discard the excess fat. Return the duck to the pan and continue to brown it. If the fat begins to smoke or the skin starts to burn, lower the heat. With tongs, turn the breasts in the pan and sear for 2 to 3 minutes more, or until browned.

Place the skillet in the oven. Roast for 5 to 15 minutes, or until a meat thermometer inserted into the center of the breast registers 135°F for medium rare, 140°F for medium. Transfer to a plate, cover loosely with foil, and let rest for 8 minutes.

Spoon off all but a thin layer of fat from the pan. Return to medium heat. Add the shallots and cook, stirring for 30 seconds. Add the wine, stock, and cranberries. Bring to a boil and cook for 4 minutes, or until the liquid reduces by about half. Stir in the vinegar, sugar, and rosemary. Taste for seasoning and add more salt and pepper, if you like.

Over medium heat, warm the apples for about 1 minute. Divide them among 4 plates. Cut the duck on the diagonal into thin slices. Place one-fourth of the duck slices on each plate and drizzle with the pan sauce.

FOR THE APPLES

2 tablespoons unsalted butter

2 tablespoons sugar

2 Honey Crisp or Pink Lady apples, cored and cut in ½-inch thick wedges

2 tablespoons lemon juice

FOR THE DUCK

2 Moulard duck magret half-breasts (each about 1 pound)

Salt and pepper, to taste

2 small shallots, finely chopped

¾ cup red wine

¾ cup chicken stock

½ cup dried cranberries

½ teaspoon sherry vinegar

¼ teaspoon sugar

1½ teaspoons chopped fresh rosemary

⅓ cup dried cranberries

Grilled Beef Kebabs with Cranberry Barbecue Sauce

If you are looking for a barbecue sauce that is tart and sweet and a bit out of the ordinary, make it with cranberries. Although grilling season and cranberry season don't coincide on the calendar, frozen berries are perfectly acceptable here.

Unlike some long-simmering homemade barbecue sauces, this one takes less than 20 minutes and produces stellar results. In this kebab recipe, the sauce is not really a marinade because you toss the beef with a small amount of sauce before skewering, and apply the rest at the end. If you add more initially, it will burn off on the grill.

You would be hard-pressed to find a better alternative for beef kebabs than sirloin tips if you are looking for a cut that will deliver lots of flavor and still be relatively tender. Tenderloin, an expensive cut, is easy to overcook and becomes dry. Though cheaper and more flavorful, chuck will be too chewy. Sirloin tip is also known as flap steak outside of New England (cut from the bottom sirloin butt.)

Serves 4

In a small saucepan over medium heat, stir together the cranberries, onion, orange juice, brown sugar, molasses, vinegar, Worcestershire sauce, jalapeno, paprika, and salt. Bring to a boil. Lower the heat, cover the pan, and simmer for 10 minutes, or until the cranberries soften. Cool to room temperature.

In a food processor or blender, pulse the sauce until it forms a coarse puree. If you would like a smooth sauce, puree a little longer.

Have on hand 12 metal skewers, or 12 bamboo skewers soaked in warm water for 20 minutes.

About 20 minutes before grilling, heat a gas grill to medium high, or light a charcoal grill. When the top coals are partially covered with ash, spread them evenly over the coal grate, and set the cooking grate on top. Heat the cooking grate for 5 minutes.

In a bowl, toss the steak with salt and pepper. Add ½ cup of the barbecue sauce and toss to coat.

On each skewer, thread 3 to 4 cubes of beef, alternating with the onion pieces.

Grill skewers for 2 to 3 minutes on a side, or until they are well seared and the center of the beef registers 125 to 130°F on an instant read thermometer. Brush with more barbecue sauce at the end of grilling.

Transfer to a platter and brush generously with the barbecue sauce. Let the kebabs rest for 5 minutes. Serve with cilantro, lime wedges, and extra sauce.

FOR THE BARBEQUE SAUCE

2 cups fresh or frozen cranberries

½ medium red onion, chopped

½ cup orange juice

3 tablespoons dark brown sugar

3 tablespoons molasses

¼ cup sherry vinegar

2 tablespoons Worcestershire sauce

1 jalapeno pepper, stemmed and sliced

½ teaspoon smoked paprika

½ teaspoon salt

FOR THE KEBABS

2 pounds beef sirloin tip steak, cut into 1½-inch cubes

Salt and pepper, to taste

1 large red onion, cut into 1½-inch pieces

Cilantro leaves (for garnish)

Lime wedges (for garnish)

Roast Chicken with Cranberry and Cornbread Salad

Once cool weather arrives, I regularly roast a chicken on Sunday nights. There is something comforting and satisfying in that routine. The leftovers go into soup, salads, or stir-fries during the week. My go-to method is to roast the chicken with lemon, as in this recipe, and throw some potatoes and root vegetables on another sheet pan to roast at the same time. Sometimes, though, I like to have a special meal, and that is where the cornbread and cranberries come in. If I happen to have leftover cornbread (even slightly stale is fine) I will use that, or I might just buy a few squares of cornbread at the market when I pick up the chicken. The pecans and cranberries go into the oven while the chicken is roasting, and the cornbread pieces toast in the oven while the chicken rests before carving.

Serves 4

Heat oven to 400°F. Have on hand a roasting pan or baking dish that is just large enough to accommodate the chicken snugly, and a 12-inch length of kitchen twine.

Pat the chicken dry with paper towels. Rub the outside all over with oil. Sprinkle the chicken liberally with salt and pepper inside and out. Place 2 lemon quarters, the garlic, and thyme inside the chicken cavity. With kitchen twine, tie the legs together snipping off the excess twine.

Set the chicken in the roasting pan with the breast side up. Squeeze the juice from the remaining 2 lemon quarters over it. Press the butter slices over the top of the breast and thighs. Wedge the spent lemon quarters under the chicken.

Roast the chicken for 1 hour and 15 minutes, or until a meat thermometer inserted into the thickest part of a thigh registers 165°F and the skin is golden and crisp.

Remove the chicken from the oven and transfer it to a warm platter. Drape it loosely with foil and let rest in a warm place for 15 minutes to allow the juices to settle.

While the chicken is roasting, assemble the salad dressing. In a bowl, whisk together the vinegar, salt, and pepper. Gradually whisk in the oil and taste for seasoning. Add more salt and pepper, if you like.

On a small baking pan, spread the pecans. Toast in the oven (while the chicken roasts) for 3 to 4 minutes, or until fragrant. Remove and cool.

continued . . .

FOR THE CHICKEN

1 (3½- to 4-pound) whole chicken

1 tablespoon olive oil

Salt and pepper, to taste

1 lemon, quartered

3 garlic cloves, lightly smashed with the side of a knife

4 fresh thyme sprigs

2 tablespoons room temperature, unsalted butter, sliced

FOR THE CORNBREAD SALAD

2 tablespoons red wine vinegar

Salt and pepper, to taste

6 tablespoons olive oil

½ cup pecans

1 cup whole fresh or frozen cranberries

1 teaspoon honey

2 cups ½-inch cornbread cubes (from 2-3 pieces cornbread)

4 large handfuls of arugula, watercress, or other green

In a small baking dish, mound the cranberries. Sprinkle with 2 table-spoons of the salad dressing, the honey, and salt and pepper. Toss together and spread in the dish. Bake for 15 minutes (while the chicken roasts). With a slotted spoon, transfer the cranberries to a bowl, and reserve the cooking juice.

When the chicken is done, turn oven up to 450°F. Pour the pan drippings into a clear measuring cup. Skim the fat from the top.

On a baking sheet, spread the cornbread cubes. Drizzle with 3 table-spoons of the skimmed pan drippings. Bake for 10 to 13 minutes, or until browned. Remove and cool briefly.

On a large platter, toss the greens with dressing. Sprinkle with the toasted cornbread, cranberries, and pecans.

Carve the chicken into serving pieces. Arrange on top of the salad. In a small pitcher, combine the skimmed pan drippings and the reserved cranberry juice. Serve with the chicken.

Stuffed Acorn Squash with Wild Rice, Farro, and Cranberries

You couldn't ask for a more festive vegetarian alternative at your Thanksgiving table than these squash halves packed with flavor and mounded high with wild rice, farro, dried cranberries, and pecans. Be sure to look for quick cooking (pearled) farro, or be prepared to cook it much longer according to the package directions. Don't just make these once a year; you will want to eat them all through the fall and winter with a bowl of soup or salad when meat takes a back seat at a meal.

Serves 6

Heat oven to 375°F. Line a baking sheet with parchment paper. Lightly oil a baking dish large enough to accommodate the squash.

On the baking sheet, place the squash halves with their cut sides down. Roast for 30 to 35 minutes, or until tender. Remove and let cool for 15 minutes. Scoop out the seeds and pulp. Cut a sliver from the bottom of each squash half so that it will stand upright, and place the halves in the baking dish with the hollowed sides up.

Meanwhile, bring a large saucepan of water to a boil. Add a pinch of salt and the wild rice. Lower the heat, cover the pan, and simmer for 45 to 50 minutes, or until the rice is tender. Set a large strainer over a bowl and drain excess liquid from the rice.

Bring a separate saucepan of water to a boil. Add a pinch of salt and the farro. Lower the heat, cover the pan, and simmer for 10 minutes, or until the farro is tender. Set a strainer over a bowl and drain.

Heat the oil in a large skillet over medium heat. Add the onion, apple, sage, and salt and pepper. Cook, stirring occasionally, for 8 minutes, or until the onion and apple soften. Stir in the cranberries, kale, and water. Cook, stirring often, for 3 to 4 minutes, or until the kale is tender. Stir in the cooked farro, rice, and pecans. Taste for seasoning and add more salt and pepper, if you like.

Spoon the filling into the squash halves in the baking dish. Loosely cover the pan with foil and bake for 20 minutes, or until it is hot all the way through. Arrange on a platter and pass around the table, or serve each squash in a wide bowl.

4 acorn squash (about 1 pound each), halved crosswise

Salt, to taste

⅔ cup wild rice

½ cup pearled (quick cooking) farro

2 tablespoons olive oil

1 onion, finely chopped

1 apple, peeled, cored, and cut into small dice

2 tablespoons finely chopped fresh sage leaves

½ cup dried cranberries

½ cup fresh or frozen cranberries

½ bunch lacinato kale, stemmed, rinsed, and cut into thin ribbons

¼ cup water

½ cup coarsely chopped pecans

Black pepper, to taste

Stuffed Pork Tenderloin with Roasted Potatoes

Stuffing pork tenderloin and roasting it while potatoes crisp at the same time is easier than you may think, and is a terrific party dish. Don't rule it out for a weeknight though, because both the roast and the potatoes can be prepared in under an hour. Instead of tying it with string, wrap it in bacon, an added bonus for bacon lovers. The cranberries add a perky, tart surprise. The bacon wrapping adds flavor and moisture to the meat.

Serves 4

2 tablespoons olive oil

¼ medium onion, finely chopped

½ fennel bulb, finely chopped

1 tablespoon chopped fresh rosemary

1 tablespoon chopped fresh thyme

½ cup coarse fresh breadcrumbs

Salt and pepper, to taste

1 (1- to 1¼-pound) pork tenderloin

⅓ cup fresh or frozen cranberries, coarsely chopped

8–10 strips of bacon (about 12 ounces), cut in half

FOR THE POTATOES

1½ pounds small red or yellow potatoes, halved

2 tablespoons olive oil

1 teaspoon dried thyme

Salt and pepper, to taste

Heat oven to 450°F. Have on hand a rimmed baking sheet.

In a skillet over medium heat, heat the oil. Add the onion and fennel, and cook for 5 to 7 minutes, or until softened. Stir in the rosemary and thyme and cook 30 seconds more. Remove the pan from the heat, and stir in the breadcrumbs, salt, and pepper. Set aside to cool briefly.

Cut a deep lengthwise slit down the center of the tenderloin but not all the way through. Open it up like a book. Cover with a piece of plastic wrap, and with a mallet or rolling pin, gently pound it until it is of an even thickness. Remove the plastic. Spread the stuffing in a line along the center of the meat and top with the cranberries. Bring the edges of the meat together to return it to its original shape. Secure with toothpicks.

On a cutting board, lay out the bacon slices overlapping them slightly. Place the tenderloin on top with the toothpicks facing up. Removing the toothpicks as you work, wrap the bacon slices around the pork to form a log. Place the tenderloin, bacon seam side down, on the baking sheet.

Roast for 20 to 25 minutes, or until an instant read thermometer inserted into the center of the meat registers 145 to 150° and the bacon browns and crisps. If the roast is ready before the bacon browns, remove it from the oven and turn on the broiler. Broil for 3 to 5 minutes to brown the bacon. Remove and let rest for 10 minutes before cutting into slices.

On a rimmed baking sheet, mound the potatoes. Drizzle with the oil. With your hands, rub the oil into the potatoes so they are completely coated. Sprinkle with thyme, salt, and pepper and toss together. Spread on the baking sheet, cut sides down. Roast for 20 to 25 minutes, or until tender and golden brown. Serve alongside the pork.

Rack of Lamb with Cranberry Mint Relish

While a rack of lamb may be in the Hall of Fame for fancy dishes, it is surprisingly easy to prepare. Spread a crust of mustard, herbs, and garlic over the lamb, pop the racks in the oven for 20 to 25 minutes, and your elegant meal is done. Brighten the rich flavor of the lamb by serving a refreshing cranberry and mint relish with it.

Serves 4

FOR THE RELISH

Makes 2 cups

½ navel orange, ends trimmed, quartered and thinly sliced

2 thick slices lemon, cut into quarters

1½ cups (6 ounces) fresh or frozen cranberries

⅓ cup sugar

½ apple, cored and cut into small dice

2 teaspoons sherry vinegar

½ teaspoon salt

1 handful mint leaves, torn into small pieces

FOR THE LAMB

2 Frenched racks of lamb (about 1½ pounds each)*

3 large slices country bread, crusts removed and torn into pieces

1 clove garlic, finely chopped

3 sprigs fresh rosemary, chopped

½ cup chopped fresh parsley

Salt and pepper, to taste

3 tablespoons grainy mustard

3 tablespoons olive oil

In a food processor, pulse the orange and lemon slices until finely chopped (but not pureed). Add the cranberries and pulse again until they are coarsely chopped and a little chunky.

Transfer to a bowl. Stir in the sugar, apple, vinegar, and salt. Refrigerate for at least one hour, or until the sugar dissolves. Just before serving, stir in the mint.

Heat oven to 425°F. Have on hand a rimmed baking sheet. If there is a lot of fat on the lamb, trim it with a sharp knife, but leave a thin layer of fat intact.

In a food processor, pulse the bread, garlic, rosemary, parsley, salt, and pepper until the bread forms coarse crumbs. Add the mustard and oil and pulse again to mix.

Place the lamb racks with the fat side up on the baking sheet. Sprinkle each rack all over with salt and pepper. Distribute the breadcrumb mixture over the top of the meat and press it lightly with your hands to firm it into place. Roast the lamb for 25 to 30 minutes, checking after 20 minutes, until a thermometer inserted into the thickest part of the rack registers 125°F for rare, 135°F to 145°F for medium-rare.

Remove the pan from the oven and let the meat rest, covered loosely with foil, for 8 minutes while you warm the dinner plates. Carve the lamb by inserting a knife between the ribs to make chops, and set four on each plate. Serve with the cranberry relish.

A rack of lamb is a series of ribs, usually 8, from the center of the animal. In most markets, a rack of lamb is sold as "Frenched," that is, the fat cap and the fat and tissue between the bones have been removed and it is ready to cook. If it is not, ask the butcher to do it for you. New Zealand and Australian lamb dominate the market, and their taste is considered by some to be a little gamier than American lamb, perhaps because they graze on green pastures for their entire lives. American lambs are often grain-fed for a short time after grazing, and the racks are larger and pricier. Both are good.

Waldorf Salad

The classics never go stale, especially when you tweak them a bit. Dried cranberries and a tangy buttermilk dressing add a modern feel to this old-fashioned salad that is truly an entrée more than a salad. It is also ideal for a beach picnic or a mountain hike where you can place a scoop on top of an avocado half or spread the salad on slices from a wholesome loaf of multi-grain bread for a satisfying lunch with a view.

Serves 4

In a large bowl, combine the shallots, vinegar, and lemon juice.

Gradually whisk in the mayonnaise and buttermilk. Stir in the chives, salt, and pepper. Taste for seasoning and add more lemon juice, salt and pepper, if you like.

Heat oven to 350°F

On a baking sheet, spread the walnuts. Toast for 8 minutes, or until fragrant. Cool.

To the bowl of dressing, add the toasted walnuts, chicken, celery, apple, grapes, cranberries, and parsley. Stir to coat with the dressing. Taste for seasoning and add more salt and pepper, if you like.

On each of 4 plates, set 1 or 2 radicchio leaves. Top with a scoop of salad, and sprinkle with parsley.

FOR THE DRESSING

1 tablespoon finely chopped shallots

1 tablespoon white wine vinegar

1 tablespoon lemon juice, or more, to taste

⅓ cup mayonnaise

⅓ cup buttermilk

1 tablespoon chopped fresh chives

Salt and pepper, to taste

FOR THE SALAD

¾ cup broken walnut pieces

3 cups cooked and diced white chicken meat

3 stalks celery, diced

1 apple, cored and diced

½ cup halved seedless red grapes

⅓ cup dried cranberries

2 tablespoons chopped fresh parsley

4–8 large leaves of radicchio

Turkey Sliders

You can have Thanksgiving any day of the week with miniature sliders. Turkey burgers can be a bit dry and tasteless, but moistened with grated zucchini and flavored with stuffing herbs, they come to life in these small bites. You can mix the ingredients in the bowl of an electric mixer if you want to just throw the burgers together in a hurry. This recipe will make 4 large burgers or 12 sliders. You really won't be able to find anything on the healthy spectrum that compares to these for watching a big game on TV with friends. Sometimes I double the batch, shape them, and freeze half for a later meal.

Makes 12

In a large bowl, mix together the turkey, zucchini, breadcrumbs, onion, egg, lemon zest, lemon juice, rosemary, sage, parsley, poultry seasoning, cranberries, salt, and pepper.

Form the turkey mixture into 12 golf-ball-size balls, and flatten them into 2½-inch wide patties.

In a large nonstick skillet over medium heat, heat the oil. Add the patties (if they don't all fit, you will have to do this in batches). Lower the heat to medium-low and cook for 2–3 minutes on a side, or until browned on the outside and the interior temperature registers 165°F on a meat thermometer.

Spread 1 teaspoon of mayonnaise on each of the rolls. Top each with a turkey patty, a tomato slice, lettuce, and the top half of the roll.

1 pound ground turkey

2 cups grated zucchini (1–2 medium zucchini, about 10 ounces total)

½ cup soft, fresh breadcrumbs

¼ medium onion, finely chopped

1 egg

Finely grated zest of 1 lemon

2 tablespoons lemon juice

1 tablespoon chopped fresh rosemary

1 tablespoon chopped fresh sage

2 tablespoons chopped fresh parsley

1 teaspoon poultry seasoning

¾ cup fresh or frozen cranberries, coarsely chopped

1 teaspoon salt

¼ teaspoon freshly ground black pepper

2–3 tablespoons olive oil

12 small, soft rolls, split in half

¼ cup mayonnaise

3 fresh plum (Roma) tomatoes, cut into slices

⅓ head of lettuce, leaves torn

Homemade Pantry

Cranberry-Citrus Relish

No matter where we end up on Thanksgiving Day, at home or away, this relish goes with us. It is smashing on a turkey sandwich, to my mind the most important part of the Thanksgiving tradition. In addition to being staggeringly easy to make, this refreshing uncooked relish provides a welcome contrast to the obligatory cylinder of cranberry jelly. Leftovers can be folded into pancake batter or stirred into plain yogurt for breakfast.

Makes 4 cups

1 small navel orange, ends trimmed, quartered, and cut into thin rounds

1 lemon, ends trimmed, halved, and cut into thin rounds

3 cups (12 ounces) fresh or frozen cranberries

1¼ cups sugar

In a food processor, pulse the orange and lemon until coarsely chopped. Add the cranberries and pulse again until all the fruit is evenly chopped. Stop before the fruit becomes a puree.

Transfer to a bowl and stir in the sugar. Refrigerate for at least one hour, or until the sugar dissolves. The relish will keep at least 2 weeks in the refrigerator in a covered container, and can be frozen for up to 1 month.

Fig, Grape, and Cranberry Conserve

Conserve is my signature holiday gift. I make several batches in the fall and my shopping is done. Plenty of jars in my cupboard stand ready to take along to friends when I'm invited to dinner, and of course, enough for our own personal consumption. The hallmark of a conserve is its combination of both fresh and dried fruits enhanced by some kind of liqueur. Here, I combine fresh and dried figs and cranberries with fall fruits and almond liqueur. It can be slathered on toast for breakfast or stirred into yogurt. It also makes a great addition to a cheese platter. The conserve could also find its way into a jam tart, baked between layers of buttery crust, or simply spooned into a baked tart shell and topped with whipped cream.

Makes 8 to 9 (8-ounce) jars

Place 3 small saucers and 3 metal spoons in a flat place in the freezer. Wash 9 half-pint jars, lids, and screw bands in hot soapy water.

In a large, wide pot over medium heat, combine the oranges, lemon, fresh figs, dried figs, grapes, plums, fresh cranberries, dried cranberries, lemon juice, and sugar. Stir until the sugar dissolves and the liquid bubbles. Continue cooking, stirring occasionally, until the mixture begins to thicken. Once it does, stir constantly to keep it from scorching, and start testing for the jellying point.

To test: Dip a large metal spoon into the pot. Hold it over the pot so that the bowl of the spoon faces you. Let the liquid fall back into the pot. As it approaches the jellying point, two distinct drops will hang onto the rim of the spoon thickly. Spoon a small puddle of the syrup onto a cold saucer from the freezer and add a little to the spoon beside it. Return it to the freezer for 3 minutes. Draw your finger across the puddle of syrup. If the surface wrinkles slightly and the channel does not close up immediately, your conserve is ready. As a second check point, tilt the spoonful of conserve. If it looks thick and jelly-like, it is done. If it runs and looks watery, continue to cook the fruits for a few more minutes.

Stir in the Amaretto. Ladle the hot conserve into 8 or 9 clean, warm jars, leaving a ¼-inch headspace. Wipe the rim of each jar with a wet paper towel and place the lid on top. Screw on the band, but don't screw it on too tight. Store in the refrigerator for up to 3 months, process in a boiling water bath, or use the inversion method to seal the jars. (see page 68)

2 navel oranges, ends trimmed, quartered lengthwise, and thinly sliced

1 lemon, ends trimmed, quartered lengthwise, and thinly sliced

12 ounces fresh black figs, stemmed and quartered

8 ounces dried Mission figs, stemmed and quartered

12 ounces black seedless grapes, halved

1 pound prune plums or small regular plums, pitted and cut into ½-inch pieces

2 cups (8 ounces) fresh or frozen whole cranberries

1 cup dried cranberries

¼ cup lemon juice

4 cups sugar

3 tablespoons Amaretto or other almond liqueur

Peach, Orange, and Cranberry Marmalade

Since peach season and cranberry season do not often occur simultaneously, you have to play with time a little for this recipe. You can either use frozen cranberries and fresh peaches, or procrastinate for a month and freeze the peaches while you wait for cranberries to come into season. It is worth cheating the clock, since the unique combination makes a lovely pink-orange marmalade, not to be found in any market. This marmalade also makes a stellar gift to give during the holidays, and indeed, all year long until your stock is depleted.

A wide pot with a capacity of at least 6 quarts is best for making jams and preserves. They need room to bubble up as they boil, so the pot should not be full to the brim at the outset. The whole process can take anywhere from 20 to 40 minutes. Patience has a very pretty reward.

Makes 7 to 8 (8-ounce) jars

3 large navel oranges, organic if possible

4 pounds peaches

5 cups sugar

Juice of ½ large lemon

3 cups (12 ounces) fresh or frozen cranberries

Scrub the oranges to thoroughly remove pesticides and wax. Slice off the ends, quarter them through the stem ends and thinly slice them, discarding the seeds.

Bring a large saucepan of water to a boil. Fill a large bowl with ice water and set it next to the stove. Wash nine 8-ounce jars, along with their lids and bands.

Halve the peaches by cutting along the "crease" through to the pit. Twist the halves in opposite directions to release them from the pit, and then remove the pit. Working with a few peaches at a time, drop them into the boiling water for about 20 seconds to loosen their skins. Very ripe peaches will not take more than a few seconds, while others may take longer. With a slotted spoon, transfer the peach halves to the bowl of ice water for another half a minute to cool them. Pull off their skins, lay them, flat side down, on a cutting board, and cut them in ⅛-inch slices.

In a large, heavy-bottomed pot, combine the sliced oranges, sliced peaches, sugar, and lemon juice. Slowly bring the mixture to a boil over medium heat, stirring to dissolve the sugar. Raise the heat to medium-high and continue to cook, stirring occasionally until the syrup deepens in color and the peaches begin to look translucent. They will need more stirring at the end of cooking because they become heavily saturated with syrup and sink to the bottom of the pan.

When the syrup begins to thicken, add the cranberries and return the marmalade to a boil. Place two or three small saucers in the freezer and start testing for the jellying point. Dip a large spoon into the pot. Hold it over the pot so that the bowl of the spoon is facing you and let the marmalade fall back into the pot. As it approaches the jellying point, two distinct drops of the syrup hang onto the rim of the spoon thickly. Spoon a small puddle of syrup onto a cold saucer from the freezer. Put it back in the freezer for about 1 minute and test it by drawing your finger across the middle to form a channel. If the surface of the jam wrinkles and the channel does not close up immediately, your marmalade is ready.

Ladle the hot marmalade into clean jars, leaving a ¼-inch headspace. Store in the refrigerator for up to 3 months, process in a boiling water bath, or use the inversion method to seal the jars (see page 68).

Freeze Peaches for Preserving

When peaches are available but time to make preserves is not, enclose them, whole and with their peel, in a plastic bag and pop them into the freezer. When it comes time to make the jam, remove them from the freezer, spread them on a tray, and leave them to thaw for about 30 minutes. They are easiest to handle when they are partially frozen but not rock solid. At this point, the skins should be loose enough pull off easily. If not, dip them briefly in hot water.

Sealing the Jars

Bath Method

1. Fill a large, deep pot with enough water to cover the jars by 1 inch. Bring to a boil.
2. Inspect canning jars for cracks and discard defective ones. Thoroughly wash the jars in hot soapy water or run through the dishwasher.
3. Wash lids and screw bands. Use only unused lids each time to ensure a good seal.
4. Fill jars to within ¼ inch of the top (headspace) with hot jam. Wipe the rim of the jar with a clean, wet paper towel before covering with the lid. Screw on the bands.
5. Set a rack or a thick folded dish towel on the bottom of the pot of boiling water.
6. Process the jars at a gentle boil for 10 minutes. If necessary, add more boiling water to cover the jars by 1 inch.
7. With tongs, remove the jars from the water and set on a dishtowel to cool.
8. After 12 hours, check the jars to ensure they are sealed. Press on the center of each lid; it should remain concave.
9. Label and date the jars by writing on the lids with permanent marker.
10. Remove the screw bands to prevent them from rusting and store the jars for up to 1 year in a cool, dark place.

Inversion Method

My friend Bonnie of Bonnie's Jams swears by this method, and I have adapted it. While not as foolproof as the boiling water bath method, it does create a viable seal. It is imperative that the jam or conserve be very hot when ladled into the jars, and the lids immediately secured. Follow steps 1 through 4 in the boiling water preservation method. Immediately turn the jars upside-down and leave them for about 10 minutes. Turn them right side up. You should hear a pop when the jar seals. Follow steps 8 through 10 to complete the process.

Whole Cranberry Sauce

Cranberry sauce is one of the simplest sauces to make, and of course, practically the *raison d'etre* for cranberry purchases in American households around Thanksgiving. In this version, hold back ⅔ cup whole cranberries to stir in at the end of cooking so there will be some variation in the texture of the sauce.

Makes about 2 cups

In a saucepan over medium heat, stir together 2⅓ cups of the cranberries, sugar, orange zest, orange juice, and salt. Bring to a simmer, and cook for 7 to 9 minutes, or until the sauce thickens and the cranberries soften and start to pop.

Stir in remaining ⅔ cup cranberries. Remove from heat and cool. Store in the refrigerator until needed.

3 cups (12 ounces) fresh or frozen cranberries

¾ cup sugar

1 tablespoon finely grated orange zest

¼ cup freshly squeezed orange juice

Pinch of salt

Pickled Cranberries

My grandmother always kept a jar of pickled cucumbers and onions in the fridge. She could put a plate of leftovers together with a little of this and that, a few pickles, and voila! A small feast. I've taken a page out of her book and used the sweet and sour brine to pickle beets, cauliflower, carrots, red onions, and even hard-cooked eggs. A jar of these cranberries comes in handy when you need to perk up leftover roast chicken, ham, or turkey. They are the pivotal ingredient for Danish Sandwiches (page 24) to pair with smoked salmon. This pickle recipe gives you a nice size stash and you can save the extra brine to use in a cranberry shrub.

Makes 3 cups

Place coriander seeds, peppercorns, and bay leaf in a spice bag, or tie them up in a square of cheesecloth.

In a saucepan over medium heat, bring the water, sugar, vinegar, orange zest, and spice bag to a boil. Add the cranberries and return to a boil.

Lower the heat, and simmer for 5 minutes, or until cranberries soften slightly but retain their shape. Transfer to a bowl to cool. Remove the spice bag and orange zest. Store in the refrigerator for up to three weeks.

1 teaspoon coriander seeds

1 teaspoon black peppercorns

1 bay leaf

½ cup water

1 cup sugar

1 cup distilled white vinegar

2 strips orange zest (removed with a vegetable peeler)

3 cups (12 ounces) fresh or frozen cranberries

Sweets

Apple, Cranberry, and Nut Tartlets

I love the idea of baking something special and traditional during the holidays. These little pies are much like mincemeat pies, but without the "meat." When the Puritans arrived, they did not celebrate Christmas, the holiday associated with mince pies in England. Instead, these desserts would have been eaten around the time of Thanksgiving. One can only speculate, but odds are good that dried cranberries would have gone into the mix.

These would make a lovely addition to a holiday table. I like to make the dough and filling on one day and fill and bake them on another day, to break up the work. You could freeze them in the muffin tin if you want to make them ahead of time, and you could even double the recipe and give some as gifts. If you take them from the freezer to the oven, allow a little more time for them to bake.

Makes 12 tartlets

In a food processor, combine the flour, sugar, salt, and butter. Pulse until the mixture resembles coarse crumbs. Add the eggs and pulse until the dough comes together in large clumps.

Turn the dough onto the counter and divide into 2 pieces. Shape each piece into a rectangle, wrap in foil, and refrigerate for 2 hours, or until ready to use (up to 3 days.)

In a large skillet over medium heat, melt the butter. Add the apples, currants, cranberries, orange peel, almonds, sugar, five-spice powder, salt, lemon zest, and lemon juice. Cook, stirring often, for 8 to 10 minutes, or until the apples soften. Remove from the heat and stir in the vanilla and rum. Cool completely.

Remove the dough from the refrigerator and allow to soften for 10 minutes. Lightly butter the cups and rims of a standard size muffin tin. Have on hand 2 baking sheets, parchment paper, a 4-inch round pastry cutter, and a 3-inch round pastry cutter. Heat oven to 375°F.

Between 2 pieces of lightly floured parchment, roll one rectangle of dough to a thickness of ⅛ inch. Transfer to a baking sheet and refrigerate for 10 minutes. Repeat with the second rectangle of dough.

Remove one sheet of dough from the refrigerator. Remove the top parchment paper, and cut out 4-inch rounds. Gather the scraps, re-roll them, and cut them into more rounds to make a total of 12 rounds. Fit the rounds into the muffin cups.

FOR THE PASTRY

3 cups flour

5 tablespoons sugar

¼ teaspoon salt

1 cup plus 2 tablespoons (2¼ sticks) unsalted butter, diced

2 eggs, beaten to mix

FOR THE TARTLETS

2 tablespoons unsalted butter

3 cooking apples, such as Honey Crisp or Golden Delicious, peeled, cored, and cut into small dice

½ cup currants

½ cup dried cranberries

½ cup diced candied orange peel

½ cup slivered almonds

⅓ cup brown sugar

1 teaspoon five-spice powder

¼ teaspoon salt

1 teaspoon finely grated lemon zest

(continued on next page)

Juice of ½ lemon

1 teaspoon vanilla extract

2 tablespoons Meyer's rum

Butter (for the muffin cups)

1 egg, lightly beaten

Flour (for rolling)

Confectioners' sugar (for sprinkling)

Divide the filling among the muffin cups. Brush the edges of the dough with the beaten egg.

Remove the second sheet of dough from the refrigerator. Remove the top parchment paper, and cut out 3-inch rounds. Gather the scraps, re-roll them, and cut them into more rounds to make a total of 12 rounds. Use a pastry tip or small cutter to cut a hole in the center of each round, or make a small cross with the tip of a paring knife. Top each filled muffin cup with a pastry round and press the edges to seal. Brush the tops with the remaining egg.

Bake for 30 to 35 minutes, or until the pastry is lightly golden. Remove and set on a wire rack to cool. When cool, remove the tarts from the muffin tin and sprinkle with confectioners' sugar.

What is a Bain-Marie?

If you have never baked using the *bain-marie* (hot water bath) technique that is used in the next recipe, don't be intimidated. Set the pudding dish in a larger pan (like a roasting pan or large baking dish) and pull an oven rack out a few inches. Place the pan on the rack. Pour enough hot water into the roasting pan—it doesn't have to be boiling—to come about halfway up the sides of the pudding dish. Carefully slide the oven rack into place. The hot water acts as insulation and allows the custard to cook ever-so-gently for a dreamy, creamy consistency. When you remove the pan, use oven mitts to carefully remove the pudding dish from the water bath to cool.

Bread and Butter Pudding

Hmm, three of my favorite food groups—bread, butter, and pudding—all in one dish. Thank you, thrifty house-wives of the thirteenth century or earlier, for creating this pudding. There's little mystery to its survival: It's just plain good and so satisfying.

Don't waste that half a loaf sitting on your counter, which will turn to stone by tomorrow's breakfast. Instead, make this supremely comforting dessert. (You can also slice and bag the bread and stash it in the freezer for a future pud-ding; if it's a little stale, so much the better to absorb the custard.) Little bits of tart dried cranberries, candied orange peel, and candied ginger punctuate the creamy pudding. Serve it warm or cold, as you like. Some thick cream on the side would be a nice addition.

Serves 6

Butter a shallow 2-quart baking dish. Have on hand a roasting pan into which the baking dish will fit. Heat oven to 350°F.

Spread the butter on the bread slices. Cut each slice in half on the diag-onal and then again into quarters to make triangles. (If using baguette slices, butter each slice.) In the baking dish, arrange the bread in over-lapping layers. Tuck the cranberries, orange peel, and ginger between the slices.

In a medium bowl, whisk the eggs, egg yolks, sugar, and salt until blended. Stir in the milk, cream, and vanilla and pour the mixture evenly over the bread. With a spatula, press the bread down into the custard and set it aside for 15 minutes to allow the bread to absorb the custard.

Gently press the bread into the custard again. Set the pudding dish inside a roasting pan. Pull out the center oven rack by about 6 inches. Set the pan on the rack, and pour enough very hot tap water into the roasting pan to come halfway up the sides of the pudding dish. Carefully slide the rack into place. Bake for 40 minutes, or until the pudding starts to brown and is slightly quivery in the center.

In a small saucepan over low heat or in a microwave-safe cup, warm the marmalade or jam.

Remove the pudding from the oven. With a pastry brush, dab the pud-ding with the marmalade and return it to the oven for 5 to 10 minutes, or until the custard is set and the bread is golden and slightly puffy. Remove from the water bath and let rest for 15 minutes or longer. Serve warm or cold, with cream or crème fraiche, if you like.

Butter (for the baking dish)

3 tablespoons unsalted butter, softened

6 slices good quality, sturdy white bread, or ½ baguette, sliced

2 tablespoons dried cranberries

2 tablespoons diced candied orange peel

2 tablespoons diced candied ginger

3 eggs

2 egg yolks

¼ cup sugar

Pinch of salt

1½ cups whole milk

1½ cups heavy cream

1 teaspoon vanilla extract

3 tablespoons orange marmalade or apricot jam

Cream or crème fraiche (for serving)

Chocolate Fruit and Nut Bars

The possibilities of toppings for these bars are open ended. If you have some nuts, fruit, and chocolate around the house, you won't even have to make a special trip to shop for ingredients. Several companies (Guittard and Callebaut, for example) make bittersweet chocolate that is ready to melt in the form of chips (not the same as semi-sweet chocolate chips), and they are very handy to use. If you buy chocolate in bar form, use a serrated knife to chop it into small pieces so the chocolate will melt evenly. Nut and seed possibilities run the gamut: whole almonds, pecans, walnuts, cashews, peanuts, pine nuts, pistachios, or whatever strikes your fancy will do. As for the fruits, any dried fruit you like, chopped into small pieces, will make a good addition.

Makes 12 bars or 24 squares

8 ounces dark, bittersweet chocolate, chopped

2 tablespoons maple syrup

1 tablespoon olive oil

2 teaspoons vanilla

½ teaspoon salt

2 cups mixed, unsalted, raw nuts and seeds (such as pistachios, cashews, and pumpkin seeds)

¼ cup finely diced candied orange peel

¼ cup dried cranberries

Heat oven to 350°F. Line a 9 x 13-inch baking pan with a parchment rectangle that is slightly longer than the pan. The parchment should fit on the bottom and extend up the two short sides of the pan. Line a baking sheet with parchment.

Spread the chocolate evenly over the bottom of the lined baking pan and bake for 3 minutes, or until the chocolate melts. Remove from the oven, and use a small offset spatula to spread it in a thin layer over the bottom of the pan. Cool for 5 minutes. Freeze for 10 minutes, or until firm. Remove from freezer.

In a medium bowl, mix the maple syrup, oil, vanilla, and salt. Add the nuts and stir to coat them. Spread them on the parchment-lined baking sheet, and bake for 8 to 10 minutes, or until the nuts are browned and fragrant. Remove them from the oven and cool for 3 minutes.

Sprinkle the warm nuts, chopped candied peel, and cranberries evenly over the chocolate. Place the parchment sheet you used for the nuts on top of the bars and press firmly with your hands to embed them into the chocolate. The chocolate will start melting from the heat of the nuts. (If it does not, return the pan to the oven for 1 minute.) Freeze for 10 minutes, or until the chocolate hardens.

Using the parchment paper ends as handles, lift the chocolate out of the baking pan in one piece and place on a cutting board. Use a sharp, heavy knife to cut into twelve 2 x 4-inch rectangles. Cut each rectangle in half to form squares if you would like smaller pieces. Store for up to 1 week in a cool place in an airtight tin between layers of waxed paper or freeze for up to 1 month.

Dark, Dark Chocolate Gelato with Bourbon-Infused Cranberries

The hallmark of gelato is intense flavor, and here you have it, ladies and gentleman, with a vigorous dose of no-holds-barred chocolate. One way to achieve that intensity and really make the dominant flavor pop is to use milk instead of cream and less sugar than you would when making traditional ice cream. Bourbon-infused cranberries create a striking counterpoint to all that chocolate.

Makes about 1 quart

In a small saucepan over medium heat, bring the sugar and water to a boil, stirring until the sugar dissolves. Remove the pan from the heat.

Stir the cranberries and bourbon into the sugar syrup. Transfer to a bowl and let cool to room temperature. Refrigerate until cold.

In a small bowl, whisk ¼ cup of the milk and the cornstarch together until smooth.

In a 6-quart saucepan, stir the cocoa powder and sugar until blended. Place the pan over medium heat and gradually whisk in ½ cup of the milk, stirring until the mixture is smooth. Gradually stir in the remaining milk, corn syrup, salt, and cornstarch slurry. Stirring constantly with a heatproof spatula, bring to a rolling boil. Boil for 45 seconds to cook the cornstarch, adjusting the heat as necessary to prevent the mixture from boiling over. Remove the pan from the heat and stir in the chocolate until completely smooth. Stir in the vanilla. Cool briefly.

Fill a large bowl with ice water. Pour the gelato mix into a gallon zipper bag, close the bag, and submerge it in the ice water. Leave for 30 minutes, adding ice as necessary, until the mixture is cold.

Meanwhile, set a strainer over a bowl and drain the cranberries.

Pour the cold mix into an ice cream maker and churn until it looks like soft-serve ice cream. (If you don't have an ice cream maker, follow the directions on page 90.) Transfer half the gelato to a freezer container. Sprinkle with the drained cranberries. Top with the remaining gelato. Press the top with parchment paper. Freeze for at least 4 hours. Serve sprinkled with chopped pistachios.

FOR THE CRANBERRIES

½ cup sugar

½ cup water

1 cup dried cranberries

2 tablespoons bourbon

FOR THE GELATO

1 quart whole milk

2 tablespoons cornstarch

½ cup dark unsweetened Dutch process cocoa powder

⅓ cup sugar

½ cup light corn syrup

½ teaspoon salt

4 ounces bittersweet chocolate, finely chopped

1 teaspoon vanilla extract

Chopped pistachios (for garnish)

Cranberry Bottom Chocolate Tart

The gods could not have designed better soul mates than deep, dark chocolate and cranberries. A lightly sweetened cranberry layer is sandwiched between a chocolate crumb crust and an easy chocolate filling made in the microwave. The cranberries cut the intensity of the chocolate and create oohs and ahs of surprise. The tart can be made 1 to 2 days ahead, and dressed with whipped cream and pistachios just before serving.

Makes 1 (9-inch) tart or pie

FOR THE CRUST

1¼ cups (about 5 ounces) finely crushed chocolate wafer crumbs

2 tablespoons sugar

⅛ teaspoon salt

5 tablespoons (2½ ounces) melted unsalted butter

2 ounces (scant ½ cup) finely chopped bittersweet chocolate

FOR THE CRANBERRY FILLING

1 packet (¼ ounce) unflavored gelatin powder

¼ cup cool water

1½ cups (6 ounces) fresh or frozen whole cranberries

½ cup sugar

1 heaping teaspoon finely grated orange zest

3 tablespoons orange juice

Heat oven to 350°F. Have on hand a 9-inch tart pan with a removable rim or a 9-inch pie pan. Wrap the outside of a straight-sided measuring cup with plastic wrap.

In a bowl, mix the cookie crumbs, sugar, and salt. Stir in the butter until combined. Spread the crumbs over the bottom of the tart pan. Use your fingers to firmly and evenly press some of the crumbs into the sides of the pan. Spread the remaining crumbs over the bottom and firmly press them down with the measuring cup. Set on a baking sheet, and bake for 10 minutes.

Remove the crust from the oven and immediately sprinkle the bottom evenly with the chopped chocolate. Let the chocolate soften for 23 minutes. With a small offset spatula or the back of a teaspoon, carefully spread it over the bottom of the crust. Let cool for 10 minutes, and then chill in the refrigerator for 30 minutes, or until the chocolate is set.

In a small bowl, sprinkle the gelatin powder over the water and stir with a fork to combine.

In a small saucepan over medium heat, stir together the cranberries, sugar, orange zest, and orange juice. Bring to a simmer and cook for 4 minutes, or until the cranberries soften but still hold their shape. Stir in the gelatin. Transfer to a bowl and chill in the refrigerator for 20 minutes, or until cool but not yet set.

Spread the cranberry filling over the chocolate crust, and return the tart to the refrigerator for 25 minutes, or until the cranberries are set.

In a medium microwave-safe bowl, whisk together the sugar, cornstarch, cocoa powder, and salt until blended. Whisk in ¼ cup milk until smooth. Whisk in the egg yolks. Gradually whisk in the remaining milk. Partially cover the bowl with plastic wrap.

Place the bowl in the microwave and cook for 3 minutes. Remove from the oven and whisk the filling to distribute the heat. Return it to the microwave for 1–2 more minutes, or until you can see the mixture simmering at the edges. Remove and whisk again. The filling should be thick enough for the whisk to leave a trail. If it is soupy, return it to the microwave for 20 to 30 seconds longer. Remove.

Add the chocolate, butter, and vanilla to the bowl. With a rubber spatula, stir until the chocolate and butter melt and the mixture is smooth.

Carefully pour the hot chocolate filling over the cranberry filling. Rap the pan once or twice to settle the filling. Set on a wire rack to cool for 15 minutes. Chill in the refrigerator for 3 hours or overnight, until the chocolate is set.

In the bowl of an electric mixer, stir the cream, sugar, and vanilla together.

Beat on medium-high speed until the cream forms soft peaks. Serve the tart topped with the whipped cream and sprinkled with pistachios.

FOR THE CHOCOLATE FILLING

¼ cup sugar

2 tablespoons cornstarch

2 tablespoons unsweetened Dutch process cocoa powder

⅛ teaspoon salt

1¾ cups whole milk

2 egg yolks

3½ ounces (about ¾ cup) finely chopped bittersweet chocolate or baking chips

2 tablespoons unsalted butter

1 teaspoon vanilla extract

FOR THE WHIPPED CREAM

1 cup heavy cream

2 teaspoons sugar

½ teaspoon vanilla extract

¼ cup chopped pistachios

Making a Cookie Crumb Crust

Cookie crumb crusts are easy to make, but need a little coddling when the crumbs go into the tart or pie pan. Start by firmly pressing the crumbs into the sides of the pan so they are evenly distributed and not too thick where the rim meets the bottom of the pan. Then spread the remaining crumbs over the bottom. Pack them down with a straight-sided measuring cup covered on the outside with a piece of plastic wrap to keep the cup from sticking to the crumbs.

Cranberry Almond Skillet Cake

A cake baked in a skillet has an irresistible rustic appeal. You could use a cast-iron skillet, or any skillet you have on hand that has a heatproof handle. Ground almonds in the batter give the cake extra flavor and a moist texture.

Makes 1 (10-inch) cake

Heat oven to 350°F. Generously butter a 10-inch skillet with a heatproof handle.

In a food processor, grind the almonds and ¼ cup sugar until fine. Set aside ¼ cup almond-sugar mixture for the topping.

In a bowl, whisk the remaining almond-sugar mixture, flour, baking powder, and salt until blended.

In an electric mixer on medium speed, beat the butter and the remaining ½ cup sugar together for 3 minutes, or until fluffy. Beat in the eggs one at a time, beating well after each addition and scraping down the sides of the bowl when necessary. Beat in the vanilla.

With the mixer set on its lowest speed, gradually add the flour mixture until the batter is smooth. The batter will be thick. Scrape it into the skillet, spreading it evenly with the back of a spoon.

Distribute the cranberries over the cake and sprinkle with the reserved almond sugar.

Bake the cake for 45 to 50 minutes, or until a skewer inserted into the middle of the cake comes out with only a few crumbs still clinging to the skewer. Set on a wire rack to cool to room temperature. Sprinkle with confectioners' sugar and cut into wedges.

Butter (for the pan)

⅔ cup whole, unblanched almonds

¾ cup sugar

1 cup flour

1¼ teaspoons baking powder

⅛ teaspoon salt

½ cup (1 stick) cold, unsalted butter, cut into slices

3 eggs

1 teaspoon vanilla extract

1 cup (4 ounces) fresh or frozen cranberries

Confectioners' sugar (for sprinkling)

Lemon Sponge Pudding with Cranberries

This rich version of a favorite old-fashioned pudding delivers everything you could wish for in a dessert; it's light yet luscious, and tart enough to make your cheeks pucker ever so slightly. As the pudding bakes, it separates into two layers: a feathery cake layer on top and a silky pudding on the bottom. Serve it warm or at room temperature. (For more details about baking in a water bath, see page 74.)

Makes 6 (4-ounce) puddings

Butter (for the ramekins)

2 cups (6 ounces) fresh or frozen cranberries

1 cup plus 4 teaspoons sugar

4 egg yolks

2 cups half-and-half

Finely grated zest of 1 lemon

¼ cup lemon juice

5 tablespoons all-purpose flour

⅛ teaspoon Kosher salt

4 egg whites

2 tablespoons confectioners' sugar

Adjust the oven rack to the middle position and heat oven to 350°F. Butter six 4-ounce ramekins. Have on hand a roasting pan or large baking dish into which the ramekins will fit.

In the bottom of each ramekin, divide the cranberries. Sprinkle each with ½ teaspoon of sugar.

In a large bowl, whisk the egg yolks, half-and-half, lemon zest, and lemon juice until smooth.

In a separate bowl, whisk the remaining 1 cup sugar, flour, and salt until combined. Gradually whisk the dry ingredients into the cream and egg yolks.

In the bowl of an electric mixer, whip the egg whites until soft peaks form. Gently fold them into the batter. Divide it among the ramekins. Set the ramekins in the roasting pan

Pull out the center oven rack by about 6 inches. Set the roasting pan on the rack, and pour enough very hot tap water into the roasting pan to come halfway up the sides of the ramekins. Carefully slide the rack into place. Bake for 25 to 30 minutes, or until the tops are golden and the centers have barely set.

Remove the pan from the oven and carefully lift out the puddings (you can use jelly making tongs if you have them.) Set them on a wire rack to cool. Sprinkle with confectioners' sugar. Serve warm or cool.

Everything Oatmeal Cookies

With the addition of sunflower seeds, cranberries, nuts, chocolate chips, and coconut, these cookies have every-thing but the kitchen sink, and they are good, well, for everything—from morning coffee to a late-night treat. A friend introduced me to the concept of slicing and baking these cookies instead of spooning them onto the baking sheet as I had been doing. Now I roll the dough into fat cylinders, refrigerate, and slice it when I want some.

This method turns out to be advantageous when you unexpectedly have a troop of kids turn up at your house. You can stash the rolls in the refrigerator for up to a week, or store them in the freezer, and slice and bake when guests turn up. The size of the roll here makes 2-inch cookies, just the right size to allow for a second one with no regrets.

Makes 30 cookies

Have on hand 2 long sheets of strong plastic wrap (about 20 inches each). Line 2 baking sheets with parchment paper.

In a bowl, whisk the all-purpose and whole-wheat flours, baking soda, and salt to blend them.

In an electric mixer on medium speed, beat the butter, granulated sugar, and brown sugar together until creamy. Beat in the eggs one at a time, beating after each addition and scraping down the sides of the bowl when necessary. Beat in the vanilla.

With the mixer set on its lowest speed, blend in the flour mixture ½ cup at a time, until the dough is smooth. Remove the bowl from the mixer stand. With a large spoon, stir in the oats, sunflower seeds, cranberries, coconut, chocolate chips, and walnuts.

Turn the dough onto a counter and use a pastry scraper to help shape it into a smooth mound. Divide the dough in half. Set each half onto a sheet of plastic wrap and roll each into logs that are about 2 inches wide, rolling the logs under your palms to make them even. Secure the ends. Refrigerate for at least 4 hours, or overnight.

Heat oven to 350°F.

Using a thin, sharp knife, slice the logs into ⅜-inch-thick cookies. Set them 1½ inches apart on the baking sheets.

Bake the cookies for 14 minutes, turning the sheets from back to front for even baking, or until they are golden brown. Slide the parchment onto wire racks to cool. Bake the remaining cookies in the same way. Cool and store in an airtight tin for up to 5 days.

1½ cups all-purpose flour

½ cup whole-wheat flour

1 teaspoon baking soda

¾ teaspoon salt

1 cup (2 sticks) unsalted butter, cut into small chunks

½ cup granulated sugar

¾ cup firmly packed dark brown sugar

2 eggs

1 teaspoon vanilla extract

1 cup rolled oats (not quick-cooking)

½ cup sunflower seeds

½ cup dried cranberries

½ cup unsweetened shredded coconut

¾ cup chocolate chips

¾ cup coarsely chopped walnuts

Pear and Cranberry Sorbet

No matter how tight the space is in my kitchen, I always find room for an ice cream maker. The reasoning is simple. I can make some real knockout desserts without turning on the oven and without much mess or fuss. This sorbet is a prime example. I love the subtle pear essence that underlies the tangy cranberry flavor; neither fruit dominates, and the color is spectacular. You could try other fruits with the cranberries, such as poached apples, or pink grapefruit, or quince that has been cooked until soft. Your only limit is your imagination.

While I've indulged in the purchase of a machine, you actually don't need an ice cream maker to make this sorbet. You can freeze the base, cut it into chunks, and process it in a food processor. (If you don't have a food processor, you could let the chunks soften a bit and use a whisk and some elbow grease to whip the frozen pieces into sorbet consistency.) Choose whichever method you can manage, just do it!

Makes about 1 quart

With a vegetable peeler, remove 3 wide strips of orange zest from the orange. Halve the orange and extract the juice. Pour it into a measuring cup and add enough water to measure 1½ cups.

In a large saucepan over medium heat, bring the orange zest strips, orange juice and water mixture, cranberries, pears, sugar, and corn syrup to a boil. Simmer for 5 or 6 minutes, or until the cranberries soften and pop. Remove from the heat and let cool for 10 minutes.

Remove the orange zest. In a food processor, puree the cranberry and pear mixture until smooth.

Fill a large bowl with ice water. Pour the sorbet mix into a gallon zipper bag, close the bag, and submerge it in the ice water. Leave for 30 minutes, adding ice as necessary, until the mixture is cold. Alternatively, refrigerate overnight.

Pour the sorbet mix into an ice cream maker and churn until it looks like soft serve ice cream. Transfer to a container; press the top with a piece of parchment paper, and cover. Freeze for at least 4 hours. If the sorbet becomes too hard in the freezer, refrigerate it for about 15 minutes to soften it, or carefully soften it in the microwave for a few seconds at a time.

1 orange

Water

2 cups (8 ounces) fresh or frozen cranberries

3 Bartlett or Anjou pears, peeled, cored, and cut into large dice

1½ cups sugar

¼ cup light corn syrup

How to Freeze Sorbet or Ice Cream Without an Ice Cream Maker

Although this is a two-step method that takes longer than freezing sorbet in an ice cream maker, it is handy to know about if you don't have a machine. When the sorbet mix has chilled in the ice water bath, place the bag on a flat tray or baking dish and freeze for 3 to 4 hours, or until hard. Cut the bag open with scissors and peel back the top of the bag. With a heavy knife, cut the frozen slab into 1-inch chunks. One-third at a time, process the chunks in a food processor until the sorbet looks creamy and no chunks of ice remain. Pack in a container, and continue until all the sorbet is used. Press the top with a piece of parchment paper, and cover. Freeze for at least 4 hours, or until ready to use.

Plum, Pear, and Cranberry Crumble

Think of this undemanding dessert as a prelude to a pie. The buttery topping is as pleasing as piecrust, yet the degree of effort, not to mention anxiety, in turning out a fruit crumble is far less than when making a pie. Plums—any kind will do here—are often overlooked as candidates for baking. Their sweet and tart juices are transformed and concentrated, and with cranberries and pears in the mix, the result is rustic and charming with flavors that pop. You don't have to peel the pears, and you could make this in a large baking dish if you want to skip the ramekins, but I think everyone should get her own little portion.

Makes 6 individual crumbles

In a food processor, combine the flour, sugar, cinnamon, salt, baking powder, and butter.

Pulse the machine in short bursts until the mixture looks crumbly and is the color of cinnamon toast.

Heat oven to 350°F. Butter six 8-ounce ramekins. Have on hand a baking sheet.

For the filling, mix the flour, sugar, salt and cinnamon in a small bowl until blended.

In a large bowl, toss together the plums, pears, and cranberries. Sprinkle with the flour mixture and toss until combined. Add the vanilla and toss again.

Divide the fruit among the buttered ramekins. Top each with the crumble topping and sprinkle with the almonds. Set on a baking sheet. Bake for 50 to 55 minutes, or until the fruit juices bubble and the topping is golden. Serve warm with cream or a scoop of vanilla ice cream.

FOR THE TOPPING

1½ cups flour

⅔ cup packed dark brown sugar

1 teaspoon ground cinnamon

⅛ teaspoon salt

⅛ teaspoon baking powder

10 tablespoons (1¼ sticks) cold, unsalted butter, cut into slices

FOR THE FILLING

Butter (for the ramekins)

1 tablespoon flour

⅓ cup dark brown sugar

A pinch of salt

½ teaspoon cinnamon

1½ pounds plums, halved, pitted, and cut into wedges

4 Bartlett or Anjou pears, cored and cut into 2-inch pieces

1½ cups (6 ounces) fresh or frozen cranberries

1 teaspoon vanilla extract

½ cup sliced almonds

Heavy whipping cream or vanilla ice cream (for serving)

Sugared Cranberries

These sparkling sugar-coated cranberries are real eye poppers. They make a sweet garnish for cakes, cupcakes, and other desserts. You can also set them out for a little sweet treat to punctuate a meal, or serve with tea and a few cookies.

Makes 2 cups

¾ cup water

1½ cups sugar

2 cups (8 ounces) fresh or frozen cranberries

In a medium saucepan over medium heat, bring the water and 1 cup sugar to a boil, stirring to dissolve the sugar. Add the cranberries. Transfer to a bowl and cool to room temperature.

Weight the cranberries with a plate to keep them submerged in the sugar syrup and refrigerate overnight.

Set a wire rack over a rimmed baking sheet. Line a second baking sheet with parchment paper.

With a slotted spoon, transfer the cranberries to the rack and spread them out so they do not touch each other. Let dry for 1 hour.

On a dinner plate, spread the remaining ½ cup sugar. One handful at a time, roll the cranberries in the sugar. Spread them on the parchment-lined baking sheet and let dry for 1 hour. Use immediately, or store them, uncovered, at room temperature for up to 2 days.

Upside-down Gingerbread with Apples and Cranberries

Gingerbread is so old-fashioned, I often forget all about it. But it's a great little cake to take to a potluck supper or a book group. The apples and cranberries, baked on the bottom of the pan and then turned upside down, take gingerbread to a new level.

Makes 1 (9-inch square) cake, or 9 squares

FOR THE APPLES AND CRANBERRIES

Butter (for the baking pan)

5 tablespoons brown sugar

2 tablespoons unsalted butter

1½ baking apples, peeled and cut into ¼-inch-thick slices

½ cup (2 ounces) fresh or frozen cranberries

FOR THE CAKE

1¼ cups flour

2 teaspoons ground ginger

½ teaspoon ground cloves

½ teaspoon ground cinnamon

¾ teaspoon baking powder

½ teaspoon salt

¼ teaspoon baking soda

½ cup (1 stick) unsalted butter, at room temperature

½ cup light or dark brown sugar

2 eggs

⅓ cup molasses

¼ cup coffee, at room temperature

Heat oven to 350°F. Butter a 9-inch square pan and line the bottom with parchment paper. Press the paper into the pan, and flip it over so the buttered side is up. Sprinkle 3 tablespoons of the brown sugar over the bottom.

In a large skillet over medium heat, melt the unsalted butter. Add the remaining 2 tablespoons brown sugar and stir until the mixture bubbles. Add the apples to the pan, and turn the heat to medium-high. Cook, swirling the pan occasionally and turning the apples with tongs, for 4 minutes or until they are lightly caramelized but still hold their shape. Transfer to a large plate to cool.

Arrange the apple slices in one layer in the bottom of the pan, with the prettiest sides down. Nestle the cranberries alongside the apples.

In a bowl, whisk the flour, ginger, cloves, cinnamon, baking powder, salt, and baking soda until blended.

In the bowl of an electric mixer on medium speed, beat the butter and brown sugar together until smooth. One at a time, beat in the eggs, scraping down the sides of the bowl with a rubber spatula as necessary.

With the mixer on low speed, beat in the molasses and coffee, and mix to blend.

Gradually add the flour mixture, and continue to mix on low speed, until the batter is smooth. Scrape down the sides of the bowl often with a rubber spatula.

Distribute large spoonfuls of batter over the apples and cranberries in the pan. Spread the batter evenly over them, taking care not to disturb the fruit. Bake for 30 minutes, or until a toothpick inserted into the center of the cake comes out clean. Remove the pan from the oven and let rest for 2 minutes.

Run a knife around the edge of the pan. Invert a serving plate on top. Use oven mitts to grasp both the plate and the pan with two hands. Flip the cake over and allow it to drop onto the plate. Peel off the parchment paper.

When cooled slightly, cut the cake into squares with a serrated knife and serve.

Victoria Sponge with Lemon Curd and Sugared Cranberries

Once favored by Queen Victoria and thus dubbed Victoria sponge cake in the British Isles, this cake provides an excellent foil for almost any filling. It is not a true sponge cake since it contains butter, cream, and leavening, but it has an airy texture and is not too sweet. It is the kind of cake to serve to your Great Aunt Margaret when she comes to tea, or to enjoy at the end of a special meal. As cakes go, it is easy enough to put together. Lemon curd is the perfect filling for the cake and you can make your life easier by purchasing it. Cream whipped with sour cream for the topping has a subtle tang. It is a bit thicker than plain whipped cream and has more staying power. The sugared cranberries on top are the crowning glory.

Makes 1 (9-inch) layer cake

Position a rack in the center of the oven. Heat oven to 350°F. Butter two 8-inch cake pans. Line the bottoms with 2 circles of parchment paper.

In a bowl, whisk the flour, baking powder, and salt until combined.

In the bowl of an electric mixer on high speed, beat the eggs for 30 seconds. Gradually stream in the sugar, and beat for 4 to 5 minutes more, or until very thick and light in color. Beat in the vanilla.

Remove the bowl from the stand. With a spatula, fold the flour mixture gently into the batter, one half at a time, fully incorporating it after each addition. Fold in the melted butter.

Divide the batter between the prepared pans. Rap them on the counter to level them and release any large air bubbles. Bake for 25 to 28 minutes, or until a skewer inserted into the center of the cake comes out clean. Set the cake on a rack to cool for 10 minutes.

Slide a knife around the edges of the pans and invert the layers onto the rack. Peel off the paper, turn the cake right side up, and cool completely.

In the bowl of an electric mixer, whip the cream, sour cream, sugar, and vanilla together just until soft peaks begin to form. To prevent over whipping, remove the bowl from the stand and use a few strokes of a wire whisk to finish whipping to soft peaks.

Set a cake layer on a plate with the top facing down. Spread with the lemon curd. Top with the second layer, this time with the top facing up. Spread the top with the whipped cream and decorate with sugared cranberries.

FOR THE CAKE

Butter (for the cake pan)

1½ cups flour

1½ teaspoons baking powder

¼ teaspoon salt

5 eggs, at room temperature

1 cup sugar

1 teaspoon vanilla extract

½ cup (1 stick) melted and cooled unsalted butter

TO ASSEMBLE THE CAKE

¾ cup heavy whipping cream

¾ cup sour cream or crème fraiche

4 teaspoons sugar

½ teaspoon vanilla

1 cup lemon curd (store-bought or homemade)

Sugared cranberries (for garnish) (see page 94)

Drinks

Cosmopolitan

Here it is: the quintessential cranberry cocktail!

MAKES 1 DRINK

Fill a stemmed cocktail glass with ice to chill it.

In a shaker, shake together the vodka, orange liqueur, cranberry juice, and lime juice. Shake until cold.

Discard the ice and strain the cocktail into the chilled glass.

Garnigh with a lime twist.

1½ ounces (3 tablespoons) vodka

¾ ounce (1½ tablespoons) orange liqueur, such as Triple Sec

¾ ounce (1½ tablespoons) cranberry juice

Juice of ½ lime, strained

Lime twist (for garnish)

Cranberry French 75

The French 75, popularized in the 1920s, was the very first cocktail I tried when I reached drinking age, sipped in a posh New York bar. I love this variation for a holiday cocktail. You could multiply the still ingredients to make punch for a group. Chill until cold and top the mixture off with champagne just before serving.

Makes 1 drink

1 ounce (2 tablespoons) gin

½ ounce (1 tablespoon) fresh lemon juice

½ ounce (1 tablespoon) cranberry syrup

2 ounces (4 tablespoons) chilled champagne

Lemon twist

In a cocktail shaker filled with ice, shake the gin, lemon juice, and cranberry syrup.

Strain into a chilled champagne flute, top with champagne, and garnish with a lemon twist.

Cranberry Hot Toddy

Clear up your cold symptoms with one of these before bed, or just enjoy this hot drink on a frigid night.

MAKES 1 DRINK

½ ounce (1 tablespoon) cranberry syrup

1 ounce (2 tablespoons) whiskey, bourbon, or other brown liquor of your choosing

6–8 ounces boiling water

1 large lemon wedge

In a mug, stir together the cranberry syrup and whiskey.

Bring a kettle of water to a boil. Pour hot water (to taste) into the mug. Squeeze the lemon wedge into the cup and stir.

Did You Know?

Ninety-five percent of all cranberries harvested are used to make juice, cranberry sauce, and dried cranberries. Only five percent are sold fresh.

Cranberry Syrup

A simple syrup infused with cranberries is the basis for flavoring all kinds of drinks. Add a bit to sparkling water and serve over a tall glass of ice for a quick afternoon pick-me-up, or use it to flavor your favorite cocktail.

MAKES 1½ CUPS

In a saucepan over medium heat, bring the sugar and water to a boil, stirring to dissolve the sugar. Add the cranberries and simmer for 10 minutes, or until the cranberries soften and pop. Cool to room temperature.

Set a fine-meshed strainer over a bowl and strain. Discard the cranberries. Transfer the syrup to a jar and store in the refrigerator. Cranberry syrup should keep for about 3 weeks in the refrigerator.

1¼ cups sugar

1¼ cups water

2 cups (8 ounces) fresh or frozen cranberries

A Cranberry Shrub

What do Babylonians, Romans, and American colonists have in common? They all drank some form of shrub. No, not a bush, but vinegar infused with fruit and mixed with sugar and water to make a refreshing drink. They were popular during Prohibition, and lately can be found on some bar menus, spiked with booze to make a cocktail. For an invigorating non-alcoholic drink, just mix with sparkling water and pour over ice.

MAKES 1 DRINK

Fill a tall glass with ice. Add the vinegar syrup and top off with bubbly water. Stir and enjoy.

1–2 tablespoons syrup from pickled cranberries

Club soda or sparkling water

Ye Olde Drugstore Cranberry Lime Rickey

Back in the day when Mom and Pop drugstores served sandwiches and sodas at a soda fountain counter, this non-alcoholic drink was a mainstay in New England. The original lime rickey, spiked with gin, was invented in Washington, D.C. in the 1880s. You could add bourbon or gin to this non-alcoholic cranberry version, or just substitute white wine for some of the bubbly water for a low-alcoholic spritzer.

Makes 1 drink

In a tall glass, stir cranberry syrup and lime juice together. Fill the glass with ice.

Top with club soda and stir.

1½ ounces (3 tablespoons) cranberry syrup

1 ounce (2 tablespoons) lime juice

6–8 ounces club soda

Nantucket Sunrise

This cocktail should really be called a Nantucket Sunset because it's just the thing to sip at the end of the day with an ocean view.

Makes 1 drink

1 ounce (2 tablespoons) tequila

6 ounces (¾ cup) freshly squeezed orange juice, strained of pulp

½ ounce (1 tablespoon) cranberry syrup

Orange twist

Into a tall glass filled with ice, pour the tequila and orange juice.

Slowly stir in the cranberry syrup. Garnish with an orange twist.

Index

Acknowledgments

Any book, especially a cookbook, has a long trail of skillful and wise friends and colleagues behind it. Years of working with great cooks underpin each recipe, and I am indebted to many for arriving at this book.

I am deeply grateful to Sheryl Julian, former food editor at *The Boston Globe,* who schooled me in the art of recipe writing with her sure and unflinching hand. She tolerated my early attempts at food photography, and helped refine my rambling recipe writing style. In addition, Sheryl was responsible for my taking this project on. Above all, Sheryl has become a dear friend and collaborator extraordinaire, and I look forward to our further cooking adventures.

To those who helped bring this book about please accept my gratitude: Amy Lyons, my editor at Globe Pequot Press, who made a special effort to foster this book; Carol Magee of the Vineyard Open Land Foundation, who explained the ins and outs of the history of cranberry growing and guided me through the bog restoration project on Martha's Vineyard; and Barbara Araujo of Squanit Bog in East Freetown, MA for inviting me to witness firsthand the wet harvest of the organic bog she operates.

I also owe a tremendous debt to the hand-holders who have bolstered me through thick and thin, especially Cassie Berry Fagen, whose smarts and wisdom are only surpassed by her good and loyal heart. To Cynthia Anderson, my rock, to Nancy Barcelo, the very best listener a friend could have, and to Ann Saybolt, my inspiring photography pal and BFF, thank you for your friendship.

Of course, thanks go to my family: to my son Luke Vargas, to Chelsea Radler, and to my husband Frank Vargas, thank you for your encouragement and your superb and appreciative taste testing.

About the Author

SALLY PASLEY VARGAS is a freelance writer and the author of *Food for Friends* and *The Tao of Cooking.* She launched her culinary career as a line cook at Rudi's Big Indian Restaurant near Woodstock, New York. Her country neighbor at the time, Chef Eugene Bernard, was teaching at The Culinary Institute of America (C.I.A.). He frequently visited the kitchen to advise and mentor the cooks, and eventually arranged for Vargas to intern with pastry chef Albert Kumin at the C.I.A. She is a cooking teacher, coach, recipe developer, and currently writes the column "The Confident Cook" for the *Boston Globe* along with seasonal recipes for the Wednesday Food Section. Vargas has written for *Vegetarian Times* and *The Magazine of Yoga.* She also contributes to *Craving Boston*, the WGBH Public Television website. Her interest in photography has led Vargas to combine her love of cooking with photos of beautiful food.